THE STORY OF
KEW GARDENS
IN PHOTOGRAPHS

THE STORY OF
KEW GARDENS
IN PHOTOGRAPHS

LYNN PARKER AND KIRI ROSS-JONES

Kew
ROYAL BOTANIC GARDENS

ARCTURUS

ACKNOWLEDGEMENTS

We have drawn on the knowledge and experience of many of our Kew colleagues and would like to thank all of these for their assistance and support. In particular we would like to thank the following for helping locate images: Barbara Lowry, Trishya Long, Stephanie Rolt, Emma Latham, Elisabeth Thurlow and Marie Humphries. To our colleagues Julia Buckley, Marilyn Ward, Lorna Cahill and our other Library, Art and Archives colleagues, who along with the above mentioned have been kept extremely busy whilst we have been working on this book! To Fiona Ainsworth, Jonathan Farley and all our other colleagues who have helped with the proof reading. To Stewart Henchie, Nigel Hepper, Martin Staniforth and Mark Nesbitt for letting us pick their brains and sometimes their photographic collections.

A special thank you to Paul Little for dealing with the deluge of photographic requests and to Andrew McRobb. To Hina Joshi for her help with the cover design. To Gina Fullerlove and Tessa Rose and their teams for their input and expertise and turning the idea into a reality. And a big thank you to Christopher Mills, for providing the idea behind the book, reading our many edits, keeping a calm head and enabling us to have the time to work on such an interesting project. And finally we would like to thank Andrew Davis and Raymond and Dominic Weekes.

ARCTURUS

This edition published in 2013 by Arcturus Publishing Limited
26/27 Bickels Yard, 151–153 Bermondsey Street,
London SE1 3HA

ISBN: 978-1-78212-059-9
AD002535EN

Printed in China

Contents

Introduction

This book is not a comprehensive history of Kew, but rather seeks to reveal stories of a much-loved garden through its photographic collections. For some it will evoke fond memories of a place well known, while for others it will provide the chance to encounter Kew for the first time.

The blossoming of the Royal Botanic Gardens, Kew, into a public institution in 1841 coincided with the arrival of photography, and through this book we witness the development of both. Photography was introduced to the public in the first half of the 19th century, born out of the experimentations of inventors such as William Henry Fox Talbot in England and Louis-Jacques-Mandé Daguerre in France. While this new, constantly evolving technology was to become the ideal tool to chronicle a rapidly changing era, Fox Talbot initially used it to explore his passion for botany, disclosing that the first subjects of his photogenic drawings were 'flowers and leaves'.

There are many stories to be told, charting Kew's evolution into a major public institution through its landscape and architecture, but also through its staff and visitors. Many of these photographs have never before been published, and through this book we are pleased to share them with a wider audience. The photographs document periods of expansion, prosperity and adversity and place Kew in an international context through its colonial links and response to global conflict and the aftermath.

Kew's substantial photographic collections have been gathered from a number of different sources, from commercial postcards to expedition albums, spread across the Archive and Art collections. Kew's first official photographer, Gerald Atkinson, joined Kew in 1922; before this time, self-employed photographers were commissioned to capture the gardens for a range of purposes, producing postcards and illustrations for publications such as *The Journal of the Kew Guild*. The largest influx of images came in 1928, when Kew purchased 5000 negatives from the photographer Edward Wallis, and this now forms the core of the historic collections. During the 1960s, the Gardens established a photographic unit, which still contributes new material to the collections.

In the days preceding photography, naturalists would sketch the plants that they botanised, the landscapes they witnessed and the different cultures they encountered. As the new medium of photography emerged during the 19th century, so botanists gained access to a fresh way of documenting their experiences. In the early years of photography, equipment was heavy and cumbersome; glass negatives were easily damaged and vulnerable to light exposure and insect attack, and the cameras themselves were susceptible to moisture damage. Later, even as equipment became more portable and easier to use, many of the same difficulties remained. Yet while drawing continued to be an important tool in the plant-hunters' oeuvre, and is still the preferred medium with which to record specimens, the photographs that were brought back provide us with a valuable

insight into what life was like in the field.

Photographic collections have also been a valuable teaching tool at Kew in the Museums of Economic Botany and, later, in the School of Horticulture, both of which have amassed large and varied picture libraries. The latter's slide library includes images of horticultural practice as well as student life, while the Museums' collections are a mixture of images of colonial botanic gardens, photographs by private individuals and records of economic crops and plantations taken by government employees, as well as promotional material provided by industry.

This book contains a selection made from the thousands of images held at Kew, intended to give an insight into its history in the 19th and 20th centuries. These photographs document the substantial changes and momentous events which influenced its progress as it grew from a small, private, royal botanic garden to the internationally important scientific centre and leading visitor attraction that we know today.

ABOVE

The earliest image of the exterior of the Palm House was made using the daguerreotype process, which was perfected in 1839 and remained popular until the 1850s. Images were produced on a copper sheet, thinly plated with highly polished silver, and their size, determined by the cameras used to produce them, was relatively small. Extremely fragile and particularly sensitive to being handled, the surface is mirror-like and has to be viewed at an angle. As well as being susceptible to abrasion, it is also vulnerable to tarnishing.

Constructing Kew

Kew Gardens, now a World Heritage Site and one of the most famous botanic institutions in the world, developed from a large strip-farmed field belonging to a private estate. It was neighbouring Richmond's royal connections that brought prosperity to the area from the 16th century onwards, with courtiers who wished to live in proximity to the newly constructed Richmond Palace, building resplendent homes such as the Dutch House (later Kew Palace) on land leased from the Kew estate.

The royal connection

By the early 18th century, two royals maintained residences in the area, with George, Prince of Wales (later George II) and his wife Princess Caroline moving into Richmond Lodge and his son Frederick taking over the large property in Kew known as Kew Farm. Frederick and later his wife Augusta radically changed the Kew estate, renovating the property with white stucco cladding – thus creating the White House – and expanding and landscaping the gardens.

It is Augusta who, along with Lord Bute, is credited with having established the botanic garden at Kew in 1759, after Frederick's death. Royal accounts show wages for the employment of a gardener, William Aiton, to manage the 'physick garden' at Kew and this is regarded as the founding of the Royal Botanic Gardens. During this period, Kew was transformed into a garden of note, with ambitious landscaping and the appointment of William Chambers to design a number of follies. On Augusta's death in 1772, George III inherited the Kew estate and united it with the royal estate in Richmond – hence the plural use of 'gardens' in Kew's name today.

By the 1830s, the Gardens were in decline, suffering from underfunding and lack of royal interest in botany during the reigns of George IV and William IV. In 1838, the year after William IV's death, the Treasury instituted an investigation of royal gardens under the direction of the eminent botanist John Lindley, which resulted in Kew being transferred from the Lord Steward's department to the Office of Woods and Forest in 1840, ending a century of royal control.

Hooker takes the helm

Kew was designated a national botanic garden and a director was sought to rescue it from its decline. Norfolk-born William Hooker, a keen naturalist, had secured the position of Regius Professor of Botany at Glasgow University at the age of 35, but he longed to return to the south, which he felt was the centre of scientific study, and set his sights on Kew. Hooker had powerful friends and through their influence he was appointed the first Director in 1841. His charm and diplomacy made him the ideal candidate for dealing with government officials and Kew was transformed under his leadership.

In 1844, the Palm House became the first major building project overseen by William Hooker. The existing glasshouses were decaying and not fit for purpose, heated by open fires that covered everything with soot. Decimus Burton was appointed architect, with Richard

Turner as chief engineer. In October 1845 the first rib of the Palm House was 'planted', but progress was slow and it was not until November 1848 that the last coat of deep blue-green paint was applied. The building was a great success and Queen Victoria was so enchanted that she paid three visits to the Gardens while it was still under construction.

This is the first photograph of the interior of the Palm House, taken on 24 July 1847 by Antoine F.J. Claudet, London's foremost daguerreotypist, while the building was still under construction. William Hooker, in a letter to Henry Fox Talbot dated 15 February 1848, mentions a 'daguerreotype representation . . . placed over the fire-place in my Drawing-room . . . attracts no attention'. Hooker clearly wanted to document his new palm house using the most up-to-date techniques, requesting his desire to have 'an interior view of this structure executed before any of the plants are placed in it', but was concerned about preserving any photograph made, enquiring whether 'such a representation [could] then be framed & exposed to the light without injury'. There has been some debate regarding who the two men in the foreground might be; some believe that they are William and Joseph Hooker or possibly, the glasshouse's designer, Decimus Burton, and the engineer, Richard Turner.

The landscape designer William Nesfield was employed to landscape the Gardens and developed a plan for a National Arboretum. Grouped taxonomically, more than 2000 species and 1000 varieties were planted.

In 1845 work on various vistas around the Gardens commenced, including the Pagoda vista, the Broad Walk – a gravel path from the Main Gate to the Palm House – and the Syon Vista, which was completed in 1852, opening up views of the Thames. Nesfield also designed an intricate parterre and widened the pond, providing a grand setting for the Palm House.

Although landmarks such as the Pagoda had been inherited, further new buildings and features were added. Kew's first museum opened in 1848 in a former fruit store and in 1857 a new museum designed by Burton opened, facing the Pond. The Temperate House, designed by Burton to accommodate the Gardens' increasing semi-hardy collections, was begun in 1861. Where gravel had been excavated for the House's terrace, a new lake was created.

Joseph Hooker, son of William, began his botanical career at the tender age of seven, attending his father's lectures. Having gained a medical degree at Glasgow University, he travelled to the Antarctic on the Ross expedition in 1839, as assistant surgeon on HMS *Erebus*. From 1847 to 1851 he travelled to India and the Himalayas, collecting many previously unknown genera, such as *Rhododendron*, common in today's gardens, and establishing himself as a celebrated plant collector and naturalist. In 1855 Joseph was appointed Assistant Director at Kew, a position his father secured for him on the basis that there was no one more qualified to sort, name and catalogue Kew's new herbarium collections.

Kew's early benefactors

In 1852, the amateur botanist William Bromfield left his herbarium and library to Kew, and William Hooker sought a home for these and his own collections. Space was found on the ground floor in Hunter House, on the north side of Kew Green, and the first herbarium curator, Allan A. Black, was appointed in 1853.

Further donations to the collections from distinguished botanists such as George Bentham meant that eventually a new building was needed to house the growing herbarium and library. Joseph Hooker, who in 1865 had succeeded his father as Director, petitioned the Office of Works for a new building and in 1876 work on a new extension began. The specimens were reorganized by plant family and rehoused in the two new galleries. Over time, further wings were added to provide additional space for the ever-expanding collections.

Along with the growing taxonomic collections, interest in plant physiology was developing and in 1875 Thomas Jodrell Phillips-Jodrell, a philanthropist interested in scientific research, donated £1500 for a new laboratory and equipment. The single-storey brick building was constructed in the Melon Yard, on the eastern perimeter of the Gardens. There were two rooms for plant chemistry and the budding science of microscopy and a smaller area for gas analysis. Joseph Hooker delegated responsibility to William Thiselton-Dyer, who had been appointed Assistant Director that year and who, two years later, would become his son-in-law.

In August 1879, Joseph received a letter from the painter and traveller Marianne North, daughter of one of his friends. In the 10 years since the death of her father, North had travelled across the globe, recording her journey in a vast portfolio of paintings. Now she had a proposition for Hooker; she would present her collection of more than 600 paintings to Kew, and design a gallery for them at her own expense. Hooker accepted the offer at once, and Marianne selected the site, engaging the architect James Fergusson to design and oversee construction of her gallery, which included a studio for her and for visiting artists. Today over 800 works by the artist are held in this unique gallery.

Under the leadership of these influential participants, Kew was maturing, both as a scientific hub and as a pleasure garden. Few places in the world hold such a diverse collection of iconic buildings, which shelter beneath their roofs an immense assortment of plants, knowledge and art.

LEFT

The oldest glasshouse plant at Kew is also one of the oldest pot plants in the world; *Encephalartos altensteinii*, the Eastern Cape giant cycad, a palm-like plant. It was brought back to the Gardens in 1775 from the Eastern Cape area of South Africa by Kew's earliest professional plant collector, Francis Masson. Since arriving at Kew, the plant has only produced a solitary cone, in 1819, an event that Joseph Banks witnessed the year before his death.

LEFT

Before the present Palm House was built, Kew had 10 glasshouses heated by fires that produced large amounts of soot. By the 1830s they were in a deplorable condition, particularly the first Palm House. During this period, many donations of plants were made, and suitable homes were required. Decimus Burton had previously overseen the design for the Great Conservatory at Chatsworth, and at the time was architect to the Royal Botanic Society, so was an ideal candidate to devise what is arguably Kew's most elegant structure. Construction began in 1845, and by November 1848 the first plants were moved in, the largest of the palms hauled on rollers with the assistance of a windlass.

LEFT

During the early years, the cycads and palms were housed in large pots placed on benches above the ornate iron grating. In 1854 a section of this metal floor was removed and the ground beneath excavated to accommodate the tallest palms. The new building was hailed as a success, with an entry in *Curtis's Botanical Magazine* proclaiming, 'The Palms in the noble house recently built for their reception in the Royal Gardens of Kew are beginning to feel the benefit of their translation from the old stoves, many of them growing with a rapidity almost incredible to those who do not witness it, exhibiting something of their native character, and not a few of them bearing flowers and fruit.' This *Encephalartos hildebrandtii* arrived at Kew from East Africa in 1901.

LEFT

William A. Nesfield, the leading landscape gardener of the age, was responsible for installing 12 boilers to heat the vast structure of the Palm House, via hot-water pipes under iron gratings in the floor, running the length of the building. To have chimneys rising from the graceful curves of the Palm House would have appeared incongruous, so smoke from the boilers was instead channelled away through underground tunnels some 150m (492ft) long, to a chimney situated adjacent to where the Victoria Gate is now. The tunnels also acted as a conduit for transporting fuel; until 1951, carts of coke were pulled by hand along rails. Today gas is used to heat the Palm House, while the tunnel accommodates the Palm House Keeper's office.

RIGHT

Beyond the flowerbeds that formed Nesfield's parterre, the Palm House chimney emerges from the trees. As was typical with so many Victorian industrial buildings, its function was concealed – in this case beneath the disguise of an elegant Italianate campanile or bell tower, constructed in red brick. Designed by Burton and constructed by Thomas Grisell, the structure stands at 32.6m (106ft), but its graceful lines integrate with its surroundings so that it complements rather than imposes upon the landscape.

In 1843, Queen Victoria donated 18 hectares (45 acres) of the Pleasure Garden, which was to be given over to arboriculture. The newly granted land, which also provided the site for the Palm House, enabled William Hooker to devise a plan for a much-needed display of trees and shrubs. In 1848, William Nesfield undertook the colossal task of creating this National Arboretum. The planting took three years, and William Hooker declared it to be 'perhaps the most complete collection contained in any single arboretum'. The Pinetum, added in the early 1870s, was largely the conception of Joseph Hooker, and was in its time the most wide-ranging collection of conifers in the world.

BELOW

With the Palm House finished, Nesfield undertook to devise a plan for the area surrounding it. A series of parterres – formal gardens with clipped hedges surrounding formally planted plots and gravel paths – enclosed the Palm House in a display of symmetrical flowerbeds. Each was initially assigned 'one kind of plant for the sake of colour'.

The Pagoda Vista was an integral part of Nesfield's design for this area of the Gardens. He imagined his vistas as a series of viewpoints radiating out from Burton's giant glasshouse, which would form the centrepiece of the new scheme, creating dramatic perspectives and guiding the visitor around the Gardens. Sir William Chambers, Princess Augusta's architect and tutor to the future George III, had been commissioned in the early 1760s to design the Pagoda, and had envisaged that it would be revealed through the trees as the spectator drew closer to it. In contrast, 100 years later, Nesfield created wide walkways, selecting trees for their architectural forms, planting them in pairs flanking the Pagoda Vista, allowing the spectator to observe the iconic building as they approached it.

BELOW

In 1847 a former royal fruit store was transformed into the Museum of Economic Botany, the first museum of its kind in the world. The object of the Museum was to complement the living collections by displaying products derived from them and to highlight the contribution made by plants to human life. William Hooker's own former teaching collection of textiles, dyes, gums, drugs and timbers formed the nucleus of the collections, with additional material coming in from the Great Exhibition of 1851. Government overseas staff were also instructed to send objects to the collection and Joseph Hooker contributed many artefacts, including teapots and teabricks gathered during his expedition to eastern Nepal.

ABOVE

The Museum's exhibits, housed in cases designed by Decimus Burton, were originally organized by commodity. Photographs, seeds, dried plant specimens, products and artefacts, either formed from the products or involved in the manufacture of them, were exhibited. In a case about the opium poppy for example, petals, seed heads, equipment used to collect the opium, opium balls, a Chinese chest used to store opium and opium-smoking apparatus could all be found.

THE HOUSE AND LAKE, KEW GARDENS.

ABOVE

The first Museum of Economic Botany proved so popular that it
was agreed that another museum would be built for the collections
to expand into. A site to the east of the pond, directly opposite
the Palm House, was chosen and Burton's building was officially
opened in 1857. This Museum had twice as much space as the
original and was organized taxonomically. It came to be known as
Museum No 1, with the older Museum being Museum No 2.

RIGHT

In 1863 a large collection of timbers was acquired by Kew from the
London International Exhibition of 1862. Since the Orangery was
standing empty, it was decided that the timbers would be displayed
there and the Orangery became known as Museum No 3. As the timber
collection grew, two galleries were added to the Orangery to provide
further display space, with the objects being arranged geographically.
The Orangery continued as a wood museum until 1953. The object seen
in the centre of this photograph is a totem pole from the village of Tanoo,
British Columbia. Made from red cedar, it originally formed part of the
supporting structure in an entrance to a house. The totem pole was later
transferred to the British Museum, where it can now be seen on display.

RIGHT

William Hooker was Kew's first
public Director. Although he had
always had a keen interest in botany,
William began his working life
running a brewery in Halesworth,
Suffolk for Dawson Turner, the
banker and botanist, later marrying
Turner's daughter Maria. Through
Joseph Banks' influence, William
was appointed Regius Professor
of Botany in Glasgow in 1820 and
Director of Kew in 1841. Under
William's leadership, characterized
by his hard work and affable
nature, Kew's dual identity as a
pleasure garden and scientific
institution was established. After a
short illness, William died in 1865,
aged 80, and the directorship of
Kew was passed to his son.

RIGHT

Joseph Hooker assumed the directorship of Kew
in 1865, having been Assistant Director for the
previous ten years. Although he had a medical
degree, his main concern had always been botany
and his father had paved the way for his career in
this field. Joseph was very much a research scientist
who never took pleasure in his administrative
duties at Kew and sought to limit public access
to the Gardens. Although he was described by
Darwin as 'peppery in temper' and was obsessively
hard-working, he also had a large correspondence
network with his friends and contemporaries and
was very much a family man, having nine children.

ABOVE

William Thiselton-Dyer, seen here with his wife Harriet outside Cambridge Cottage, Kew, became Assistant Director in 1875 and succeeded Hooker as Director in 1885. Previously he had taught botany at various universities. His connection with the Hookers was more than just professional – Harriet, whom he married in 1877, was Joseph's eldest daughter. A man of autocratic character, he played a mainly administrative role as Assistant Director, while as Director he focused on landscaping and opened the Gardens' first public refreshment pavilion. Throughout his time at Kew, Thiselton-Dyer maintained and strengthened the organization's involvement with the colonial gardens and botanic stations. Cambridge Cottage, the building shown here, was acquired by Kew in 1904. It had previously been the home of the second Duke of Cambridge and was opened as a forestry museum in 1910 – one of Thiselton-Dyer's long-held plans.

ABOVE AND RIGHT

When Frederick North, her father and travelling companion, died five days after her fortieth birthday, Marianne North wrote that she had decided to 'fill up my life with other interests'. To this end she married her love of travel and her talent for art in an exploration documenting all of the flora, fauna and traditions she encountered on a voyage across the world, an endeavour that would last until her death some 20 years later.

In 1879, Sir Joseph Hooker accepted Marianne's donation of her paintings and a gallery in which to exhibit them. She commissioned the architect James Fergusson, an authority on Indian temples, and together they set about formulating a design for the site. The building's red-brick façade and the inclusion of benches beneath a shady veranda evoked a colonial setting, recalling Marianne's particular love of India, while the clerestory windows lent natural light to the interior. She devised her own hanging plan, eventually completely covering the walls with 832 artworks representing more than 900 species of plants from four continents, grouped according to geographical location. The gallery opened on 9 July 1882.

RIGHT

Marianne North met Julia Margaret Cameron when she stayed at the photographer's home at Kalutara, Ceylon, now Sri Lanka. Marianne admired Julia's photography, and agreed to pose for a photograph; her account of the sitting, published in *Recollections of a Happy Life: Being the Autobiography of Marianne North*, illustrates her self-effacing nature.

'She dressed me up with flowing draperies of cashmere wool, let down my hair, made me stand with spiky cocoa-nut branches running into my head, the noonday sun's rays dodging my eyes between the leaves as the slight breeze moved them, and told me to look perfectly natural (with a thermometer standing at 96°)! Then she tried me with a background of breadfruit leaves and fruit, nailed flat against a window shutter, and told them to look natural, but both failed; and though she wasted twelve plates, and an enormous amount of trouble, it was all in vain, she could only get a perfectly uninteresting and commonplace person on her glasses, which refused to flatter.'

Sir William Chambers designed many temples in the classical style around the gardens; stylistically, the Temple of the Sun, built in 1761, reflects a resurgence of interest in Classicism, prompted to some extent by the fashion of the Grand Tour, undertaken by 18th-century gentlemen. Contemporary critics were not convinced; the *London Magazine* (August 1774) complained that 'The Harlequin temples of Confucius and the Sun, are mere baubles, and seem calculated for citizens to take their tea in'. The folly was destroyed on the night of 28 March 1916, when a ferocious storm brought one of Kew's cedar of Lebanon trees down on top of it. The storm also caused the demise of the last of the Seven Sisters' Elms, which were reputed to have been planted by the daughters of George III. The cedar originated from the 3rd Duke of Argyll's garden at Whitton Park, the best trees from his collection having been transferred to Kew after his death.

RIGHT

Designed by Sir William Chambers and built in 1762, the Pagoda rises to a height of almost 50m (164ft). Based upon the temples that Chambers had seen during a visit to China, the roofs were originally adorned with wooden dragons painted gold. Popular legend (purportedly circulated by Joseph Hooker) had it that they were actually made of gold and were sold to settle George IV's gambling debts. In truth they simply rotted away, a fact that William Aiton, who managed the Botanic Garden under Augusta, Dowager Princess of Wales, remembered from his childhood.

THIS PAGE AND OPPOSITE

In 1859 Decimus Burton was commissioned to design a
house for the Gardens' semi-hardy plants. With extensive
collections arriving from temperate parts of the world
such as Australasia, South Africa and northern India, it
had become clear to William Hooker that a building was
required to house such plants. A site near the Arboretum
was chosen and construction began. The house was to
be more than twice the size of the Palm House, covering
4880sq m (1¼ acres) and 19m (62ft) high. Unforeseen
costs caused work to be halted in 1863 and the house
was opened to the public just three-quarters complete.
It was not until 1898 that it was finally finished.

The central hall was divided into 20 oblong beds,
containing tall plants and trees, with side beds of shrubs, such
as rhododendron and camellias. Along the side ran benches
on which smaller plants in pots were placed. As construction
of the house was completed, wings containing plants from
temperate areas were added. Today the Temperate House
is the largest surviving Victorian glasshouse in the world.

Hunter House was once the residence of the Duke of Cumberland, brother of William IV. After Cumberland's death in 1851, the ground floor of the house was made available to William Hooker for his herbarium and library collections, and gradually the collections expanded into the remainder of the building. Up until that time there had not been a herbarium at Kew, and Joseph Banks' dried specimen and book collections in his own home at Soho Square were consulted by those who needed to identify and classify plants. Hooker allowed staff and select researchers to view his collections in Hunter House, and a curator, Allan Black, was appointed in 1853.

ABOVE

Kew did not have a library until 1852, when William Bromfield bequeathed his herbarium and library collection of about 600 volumes, supplemented a couple of years later by George Bentham's library of 1200 texts. Gradually, specific funds were allocated to purchase books and the library collection developed both as an archive of rare material relating to botany and as a working collection, supporting the work of the gardeners and scientists. The collections were housed in the front of Hunter House and it was not until the 1960s that a purpose-built library was constructed. In this photograph, the desk to the left is that used by Bentham, who, after donating his collections to Kew, visited daily over a period of 30 years.

ABOVE

As the herbarium collections grew, it became clear that additional space was required to house them. Joseph Hooker's request for an extension was finally granted and in 1871 several rooms at the back of Hunter House were demolished to make way for a two-storey wing. The building was functional, with wooden cabinets for storing the paper sheets to which the pressed, dried specimens were attached. The bays were designed to make the most use of natural light, since gas lighting posed a huge fire hazard for the collection. Further wings were added in 1902, 1932, 1969 and 2009.

ABOVE

The Waterlily House was constructed in 1852 to house the *Victoria regia* (later renamed *Victoria amazonica*), a magnificent waterlily named in Queen Victoria's honour. The specimen had first been propagated from seed at Kew in 1849, after several unsuccessful attempts, but it failed to bloom. The flowering of this species was finally achieved by Joseph Paxton, gardener to the Duke of Devonshire, at Chatsworth in November 1849, and the first bloom was presented to the Queen herself. The waterlily must have made a huge impression on Paxton, whose design for the Crystal Palace, constructed in 1851, was said to have been influenced by the curvilinear structure of its leaf. Kew's specimen finally blossomed in June 1850, and continued to flower for the next six months, but it never flourished in this glasshouse.

ABOVE

The T-range was a series of greenhouses that took their name from their resemblance to a capital letter 'T'. Built to house the *Victoria amazonica*, they also provided areas for orchids, ferns, and later insectivorous plants, cacti and agaves. The complex was demolished in 1983, and replaced by the Princess of Wales Conservatory.

BELOW

The girl in this photograph, taken in 1923, is identified as 'Miss Cotton' and it is likely that she is the daughter of Arthur Cotton, who was keeper of Kew's Herbarium and Library at this time. She appears more than a little apprehensive to pose on the leaf of this giant waterlily, *Victoria amazonica*, but it is said that the leaves can support up to 45kg (7st) if the load is evenly distributed.

RIGHT

This photograph of Joseph Hooker and his wife
Hyacinth is the only known image of Joseph in the
Gardens. It is believed to be Joseph's last visit to the
Gardens, and was taken after he had retired to his
home, The Camp, in Sunningdale, where he died in
1911. Joseph married Hyacinth Jardine in 1876, after
the death of his first wife, Frances, in 1874. While on
his honeymoon in Scotland, Joseph wrote of Hyacinth
to Thiselton-Dyer that 'Mrs Hooker is an excellent
traveller, climbs and walks like a mountaineer'.

ABOVE

The Rhododendron Dell began life as Capability Brown's Hollow Walk, created in 1773, and planted with mountain laurels. During his travels in the Himalayas, Joseph Hooker sent back to his father at Kew many new species of rhododendrons; Kew's annual report for 1850 refers to '21 baskets of Indian orchids and new species of rhododendrons' received. These were planted in the dell, creating stunning spring displays. In 1911, Ernest Wilson's rhododendrons were also added. Now, the dell is the only surviving piece of Capability Brown's landscaping of the Gardens.

Kew, the Imperial Garden

Following the death of her husband, Frederick, Prince of Wales, in 1751, Princess Augusta assumed governance of Kew, decreeing that it should 'contain all the plants known on earth'. Under her control, the Gardens began to engage in a more international role and later that century Joseph Banks would commission collectors to bring back specimens for the Gardens from across the world. Through his influence, Kew began to be involved in economic botany, moving commercially valuable plants around the globe. The Lindley Report of 1838 confirmed this international role, declaring that Kew should become 'the national botanic garden', providing supplies for the colonial gardens and gathering information about their proceedings, while introducing and dispersing 'new and valuable plants'.

Yet when William Hooker took up his directorship in 1841, colonial plant collecting had all but ceased. Prompted by Lindley's recommendations and concerned that Kew was losing ground, Hooker wasted no time in recruiting collectors who were dispatched to various parts of the world, sending back specimens to be propagated at Kew before being shipped to the colonial botanic gardens, of which there were about ten in 1841. Later, during his Assistant Directorship, Thiselton-Dyer described Kew as 'a sort of botanical clearing-house or exchange for the Empire'. While the main focus was on plants that could be used as economic crops to develop new industries, for example rubber, plants were also collected that would decorate the gardens of the colonial governors or provide food or medicine.

By the time of Joseph Hooker's retirement from Kew in 1885, there were about 100 colonial botanic gardens and stations in existence in all corners of the Empire. Although Kew was not officially responsible for them, it did play an important role in their establishment and ongoing management. Most of the senior staff in the colonial gardens were Kew-trained and Kew was actively involved in recruitment, recommending individuals, often its own staff, to these positions.

Kew also supplied huge numbers of plants for these gardens. To introduce a new commercially viable plant to a particular part of the world, seeds or plants would initially be sent to the local botanic station or garden for propagation. In addition, Kew provided taxonomic and horticultural expertise, identifying new discoveries and advising on cultivation.

However, the relationship between the colonial gardens and Kew was not one way; the gardens sent many thousands of specimens to Kew. These were added to the Living and Herbarium collections and were the genesis of the compilation of the floras of Australia, Tropical Africa and India. Indigenous knowledge of the plants and their uses was also passed on to Kew, who documented this information, using it to supplement current understanding and to educate the public through displays in the Museum of Economic Botany.

In his Annual Report of 1877, Joseph Hooker

referred to Kew as the 'botanical headquarters of the British Empire'. This function continued throughout the 19th and early 20th centuries, and although the emphasis gradually changed with the demise of the Empire, Kew still retained a major international role.

ABOVE

Lalbagh Botanic Gardens in Bangalore were originally established in 1760 by Hyder Ali, the ruler of Mysore. Once they came under state control in 1856, William Hooker was consulted on the recruitment of a superintendent and a former member of Kew staff, William New, was appointed. Plants were sent from Kew to stock the Gardens and Lalbagh entered into the programme of plant exchange. In the 1886 annual report, the Superintendent writes that 3750 packets of seeds and 10,945 plants were sent out from the Gardens. As well as being a horticultural hub, the Gardens were a real visitor attraction, holding annual horticultural shows. Weekly concerts were held at the bandstand in this photograph and a menagerie housed animals such as tigers, lions, bears and monkeys.

ABOVE

This photograph, taken in 1887, shows a 23-year-old China tea plant (*Camellia sinensis*), introduced into Natal from plants sent by Kew. Tea plants can remain in production for up to 50 years.

ABOVE

Harvesting tea leaves, often known as 'plucking', was frequently done by women and children and required skill. The leaves needed to be picked selectively to maintain the quality of the tea and could not be held in the hand for long, as contact caused them to grow warm and turn sour. As they were picked, the leaves were put into baskets, often carried on the backs of the pickers. An experienced picker could gather 35kg (77lb) of leaves a day. From today's best plantations, it is possible to produce yields of 1000kg per hectare (8cwt per acre).

ABOVE

Tea plantations in mountainous areas often rely on terraces to prevent erosion and to provide water for the plants.
The bushes are carefully maintained to a height of about 1m (3¼ft), with paths between them, enabling easy
harvesting. There are two main varieties of tea, *Camellia sinensis* var. *sinensis*, used to produce Chinese and green
tea (shown here, on a plantation in the Far East), and *Camellia sinensis* var. *assamica*, used for Assam (Indian) tea.

ABOVE

Once the tea had been picked, it was taken to a 'factory' for processing before it was shipped to its final destination. Tea processing consists of a number of stages, including rolling, fermenting and sorting. In the 19th century these were carried out mainly by hand, but as time went on, tasks such as rolling and sorting were mechanized. *The Tea Cyclopaedia*, published in 1882, prescribes that no broom should ever be allowed in a factory, only 'wet swaps', in order to avoid dust or ash from the drying processes getting into the tea.

RIGHT

Keeping tea fresh was a real challenge in the days before vacuum packing; once it was processed by the factory, tea might take up to a year to reach its final destination. The Indian factories copied the China tea chest, designed to keep the tea dry and to protect it from any pests or strong smells. With the demise of the East India Company, these chests were transported by tea clippers, racing to fulfil the West's desire for the freshest tea.

The first stage of the production process is the drying-out of the tea leaves, known as 'withering'. When picked, tea leaves are roughly 80 per cent moisture, which needs to be removed in order to preserve them and enhance their flavour. Here the leaves are spread out on trays or shelves in airy rooms to enable them to wither.

RIGHT

Here labourers are shown carrying tea bricks from western Sichuan in China to Tibet in 1908. The loads were about 140kg (300lb) and the photographer, plant-hunter Ernest Wilson, recorded that the men made progress of about 9.5km (6 miles) a day over 'vile roads'.

ABOVE

In 1859, Richard Spruce was commissioned by William Hooker to collect cinchona plants and seed in Ecuador, as part of a joint India Office and Kew project. The aim was to transfer cinchona from South America to India and establish the industry there. Spruce, accompanied by Robert Cross, a Kew gardener, successfully collected and cultivated 637 plants and 100,000 seeds of *Cinchona succirubra* (red bark tree), which were sent to India via Kew, where a forcing house for the germination of cinchona seeds had been constructed. By 1880, there were nearly 6070 hectares (15,000 acres) of cinchona under cultivation in southern India alone.

LEFT

Photographed on the Madulsima Cinchona Cos Estate, Ceylon (Sri Lanka) in 1882, these *Cinchona succirubra* trees are 8–10 years old and 7.6–9m (25–30ft) tall. The outer bark has been shaved and the trunks have then been covered with grass to encourage the regrowth of the bark. After quinine alkaloids were first extracted from the bark in 1820, quinine became the standard treatment for malaria within five years.

RIGHT

These seedlings of *Cinchona succirubra* were photographed on arrival in Ootacamund, southern India, on 9 April 1861. Collected by Richard Spruce in Ecuador, the plants were received by William McIvor, a former Kew gardener, who was Superintendent of the Botanic Garden in Ootacamund, where he successfully cultivated the red bark trees. This helped to strengthen Kew's role as an imperial garden – although Kew's refusal to purchase a new species of cinchona with a much higher quinine content in the 1860s led to the Netherlands' predominance in the quinine trade.

RIGHT

After the bark had been stripped from the tree it was placed on frames to be dried, forming quills as the moisture evaporated. It was important to keep the bark from different parts of the tree separate as the quills formed from younger bark higher up the tree contained a lower amount of quinine alkaloids, meaning they were less commercially valuable. Quills from the same part of the trunk would be cut to matching lengths and packed together into bags or bales, so they could be sold together. Each bale was marked with the weight, the species of cinchona and the plantation where it was grown.

Henry Ridley was director of the Singapore Botanic Garden from 1888 to 1911. On taking up his post, he found rubber trees that had been sent from Kew in 1877. Joseph Hooker had obtained the seeds from Henry Wickham, who had sent 70,000 seeds of *Hevea brasiliensis* (the Pará rubber tree) from the trees' native home of Brazil in 1876. Ridley cultivated the trees and demonstrated that they could be regularly tapped for the latex from which rubber is made. Through his expertise and encouragement, the Malayan rubber plantation industry was established and today most of the world's rubber production comes from plantations in Malaysia, Thailand and Indonesia. In this image, 'Rubber Ridley' (left) can be seen displaying the tapping of a rubber tree, releasing the latex which flows from the inner bark. On his retirement from Singapore, Ridley travelled extensively, eventually settling in Cumberland Road in Kew, where he lived until he passed away at the age of one hundred.

ABOVE

The *Kew Bulletin* for 1892 describes the process of rubber production thus: 'Rubber is obtained from incisions cut through the bark, from where the sap trickles into small bowls. It is cured by being ladled onto a paddle-shaped implement and held over a stove.'

ABOVE

Here a gang of sappers is about to set out for a day's work in a rubber plantation, equipped with the tools used for extracting latex. This image was taken in Mozambique, from where England imported 380 tonnes of rubber in 1891.

RIGHT

To tap a tree, the tapper will make a small incision in the bark with a tapping knife, removing a small piece of bark. This needs to be done with skill, as too deep a cut will damage the tree, which otherwise can be tapped many times. Once all the latex has been drained it is naturally replaced by the tree and can be tapped again.

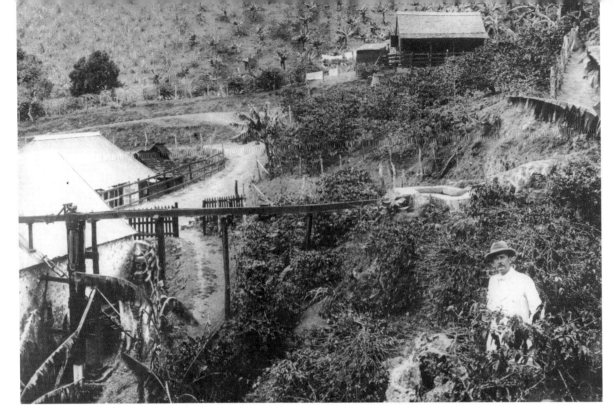

LEFT

Like cinchona, coffee (*Coffea*) belongs to the Rubiaceae family. This family was, and still is, extremely commercially important – today, coffee is the second most valuable international commodity. This photograph shows a plantation in the Blue Mountains of Jamaica, where coffee has been produced for several hundred years and is today one of the world's finest brands. Kew became involved when Daniel Morris was Director of the Public Gardens in Jamaica, sending him a variety of crops for cultivation and advising on disease and blight.

RIGHT

This image shows the coffee crop at the Batu Cave Estate, Singapore in 1899. The two most popular commercial species of coffee are *Coffea arabica*, known as Arabian, and *Coffea canephora* or *robusta*. The plant is not usually ready to harvest until the trees are about 3–4 years old, depending on species. White flowers appear, giving rise to fruit known as cherries, which ripen from green to red. The grower must select exactly the right time to pick the fruit; if it is left too long, the cherry will turn brown and dry out. The majority of coffee-producing nations harvest one crop a year, which is traditionally gathered by hand, a gruelling and labour-intensive practice.

Drying the coffee 121.

LEFT

These workers in the Straits Settlements, Southeast Asia, are shown drying coffee in 1899. Once harvested, the 'cherries' were sorted, then air dried and raked continually to prevent mildew and promote even drying. This process could take up to several weeks. Once dried, the cherries were milled, removing the husks to reveal the beans, which were then graded and packed, ready for roasting and grinding.

457 Coffee Crop, Batu Cave Estate

Cinnamon is derived from the dried bark of *Cinnamomum verum*, a small evergreen tree, and is said to be one of the oldest spices in the world. It is native to Sri Lanka, where it is still mainly grown. Here a labourer on a Sri Lankan (Ceylonese) plantation is cutting the shoots; the bushes are managed in such a way to encourage straight shoots, which are harvested once they have reached a certain height.

LEFT

The cinnamon is contained in the inner bark of the tree. Once the shoots have been harvested the outer bark is peeled off, after rubbing with a brass rod or blunt instrument to loosen it, and the inner bark is then removed and scraped clean.

ABOVE

Once the inner bark has been cleaned, the quills are placed one inside another to form quills 1m (3 1/4ft) long, which are then dried on racks. They are sorted by quality, with the best cinnamon coming from the middle of the shoot. These photographs show cinnamon production in Sri Lanka in the 1880s.

ABOVE

Pepper, another spice with a long history, is native to India. Black, white and green peppercorns all come from the same plant, *Piper nigrum*, with the timing of the harvest and subsequent processes dictating their colour. Pepper plants grow up supports and are harvested when they are about three years old and over 2m (6½ft) high. During harvest, which lasts for about three months, the fruits are picked every two weeks.

RIGHT

Originally from Mexico, hemp has been in
cultivation for many hundreds of years, for
food, fibre, oil, medicines and narcotics.
Kew's association with the plant has
been long; Joseph Banks had a keen
interest in hemp production and procured
many seeds, which were passed to the
navy to ship to the emerging colonies.
Hemp was also a key resource for the
navy itself, with the fibres being used
for sails and ropes. Later in the 19th
century Kew sent hemp seed around
the world, offering advice on growing
different types, and through stock supplied
by Kew, British East Africa became the
world's leading producer of sisal hemp.
Shown here is hemp fibre production in
Tochigi, Japan. Hemp has been grown in
Japan for many hundreds of years but this
held little interest for Kew, which focused
rather on developing the hemp industries
in British colonies. This image came to
Kew from the Japan-British Exhibition
of 1910, which was held to encourage
Japanese-British relations, particularly
regarding trade and manufacture.

The trade in cotton existed long before Kew came to prominence, and its economic value attracted Kew's attention. The India Office corresponded with Kew, enquiring how to improve the cultivation of cotton, and advice was provided on hybridization and avoiding the degeneration of the seed. Specimens were identified, and Kew sent different species to India, as well as trained gardeners. Here, a woman is spinning cotton, which originates from the soft white fibres that grow around the seeds of the plants in the bolls – the fruit of the plant.

The poppy *Papaver somniferum* has been grown for opium for many hundreds of years, and under the East India Company the export of opium from India to England grew into a thriving trade. To produce the opium, the poppy heads were pierced to collect the milk, which was then taken to factories for processing. Kew's Museum of Economic Botany No 1 displayed equipment not only for the production of opium but also for smoking it. The museum's guide explained, 'A drop about the size of a pea is roasted over the lamp and then placed over a little aperture in the bowl of the pipe; the smoker in a reclining posture keeps it alight by holding it over the flame.' This photograph, taken by Ernest Wilson, shows fields of cultivated white poppy in Eastern Sichuan.

RIGHT

The scarlet dye known as cochineal is produced from carminic acid extracted from the beetle *Dactylopius coccus*, which lives on the cactus *Opuntia*. This photograph, thought to have been taken by the renowned photographer Eadweard Muybridge, shows cochineal beetles being harvested from *Opuntia* plants in Antigua. Joseph Hooker purchased a series of six photographs from Muybridge, as well as a few more that, Muybridge writes, 'I thought might be interesting and which you will perhaps be kind enough to accept.'

ABOVE

In the 19th century Kew had close links with Singapore Botanic Gardens which are still maintained today. The latter were originally established as pleasure gardens in 1859 by an agricultural society, but the focus became more scientific when their management was passed to the government in 1874 and Kew's influence increased. Former members of Kew staff were sent and many plants were exchanged between the two organizations, including rubber trees. This image of the Gardens shows how different they were to the heavily cultivated gardens at Kew. Under the Director, Henry Ridley, similar jungle areas were transformed into plantations for rubber trees, enabling the Gardens to provide seed to the emerging rubber industry.

ABOVE

This photograph shows Henry Ridley standing outside the Herbarium at Singapore Botanic Gardens. Ridley transformed the Gardens during his 23-year tenure as Director and under his leadership they became an international scientific organization. It was Ridley who identified Singapore's national flower, *Vanda* 'Miss Joaquim'. Discovering this orchid hybrid in her garden, horticulturalist Agnes Joaquim took it to Ridley, who named it and described it in the 1893 *Gardeners' Chronicle*.

LEFT

The Hong Kong Botanic Garden is situated on the north slope of Mount Austin, more commonly known as Victoria Peak. Although parts of the Garden had been open to the public since 1864, it was formally founded in 1871, with Charles Ford as its first Superintendent. Ford collected plants in China and Taiwan, many of which he sent to Kew, and produced the *Catalogue of Plants in Government Gardens, Hong Kong* in 1876. This view of the Gardens, taken by Ernest Wilson in April 1909, shows an example of *Pinus massoniana*, standing over 20m (65ft) tall.

BELOW

Raphiolepis indica, the Indian hawthorn, is a hardy evergreen shrub of the Rosaceae family, shown here growing in Hong Kong Botanic Garden. Its white or often pink flowers make it a popular garden shrub, particularly in North American gardens. The fruit is edible when cooked.

RIGHT

The Royal Botanic Garden, Calcutta (now the Acharya Jagadish Chandra Bose Indian Botanic Garden, Kolkata) and Kew share many similarities. Both are based on the outskirts of large cities, flanked by a large river, and they have many common features, such as lakes, palm houses, herbaria and libraries. Directors of Calcutta have also been directors of Kew and there is a long history of collaboration and plant exchange. The Garden in Calcutta was founded by Colonel Robert Kyd of the East India Company in 1787 and remained under the EIC's control until 1857, when ownership passed to the government. Cinchona, rubber and tea were all trialled in the Garden, using seeds and plants sent from Kew.

ABOVE

The Great Banyan Tree in the Acharya Jagadish Chandra Bose Indian Botanic Garden, Kolkata, is now almost 250 years old and is recorded as the world's widest tree, at about 450m (1476ft). Although it appears to be formed of many separate trees, these are in fact aerial roots, developed from one single tree. This image shows the tree at the turn of the 20th century and the sign on the bench records that at this time the tree was 938ft (286m) wide.

ABOVE

The Garden had a dispensary for employees and their families, seen here in about 1910. The man dressed in white, holding a bottle, is the doctor.

LEFT

This bell was tolled to summon the labourers to work. Here it is being rung by a Nepali durwan (doorman) in about 1910.

ABOVE

Charles Frazer proposed the site that became Brisbane Botanic Gardens in 1828, and in
1855 it was formally recognized as a botanic reserve with Walter Hill as its first Curator.
One of the Gardens' most famous former residents was Harriet the tortoise, reputedly
collected by Charles Darwin during his expedition to the Galápagos. Arriving in 1860,
she resided there for more than 100 years after being given to the Gardens by John
Clements Wickham, an officer on board HMS *Beagle* during Darwin's voyage. Harriet
was eventually moved to the Australia Zoo in Queensland and lived to the age of 176.

ABOVE

The Botanic Gardens in Adelaide opened to the public in 1857, largely thanks to
the vision of its first director, London-born George Francis. The Palm House was
imported from Bremen in Germany in 1875, under the supervision of the Gardens'
second Director, Moritz Richard Schomburgk. He also oversaw the building of
the Victoria House in 1868 to house the *Victoria amazonica* which had been
discovered growing in British Guiana by his brother Robert in the 1830s.

LEFT

The Royal Botanic Gardens in Sydney are situated on land adjacent to the city's natural harbour. The Gardens were
founded in 1816 by Lachlan Macquarie, Governor of New South Wales, as part of his residence. Its first superintendent
was Charles Frazer, and in 1821 he was formally appointed 'Colonial Botanist'. Port Jackson, the area of Sydney
where the Gardens are situated, was formerly home to the indigenous Eora people, but in 1788 became the
location of the continent's first penal colony when the First Fleet landed with a transport of more than 700 convicts.
Joseph Banks had maintained a keen interest in Australian botany since joining Cook's HMS *Endeavour* voyage as
the ship's naturalist. He sent collectors to explore the region and many specimens were sent back to Kew.

LEFT AND ABOVE

St Vincent is one of the oldest colonial botanic gardens, having been
established in 1765 by General Robert Melville, Governor of the Windward
Islands, at the request of George Young, one of the colony's physicians
and the Gardens' first curator. It was to these Gardens that Joseph Banks
suggested the introduction of breadfruit as a cheap food source for slaves
on the plantations. The plants finally arrived at St Vincent in 1793 on HMS
Providence, captained by William Bligh, who had notoriously failed in his first
expedition to collect and transport the plants from Tahiti when his crew on
HMS *Bounty* mutinied. On his return journey to England, along with other
plants collected on the voyage, Bligh brought 465 pots containing plants back
to Kew. The Gardens played a key role in the introduction of many different
plants, both medicinal and agricultural, to the West Indies, as well as providing
an important link between the colonial gardens in the West and East.

ABOVE

Most of the colonial botanic gardens had herbaria, such as this
one in the Royal Botanic Gardens, Trinidad, reflecting their role
as scientific institutions rather than just pleasure gardens. Plants
were identified and recorded in these herbaria, with duplicate
and unidentifiable specimens being sent to Kew's Herbarium.

In 1894, Downing Street wrote to Kew, asking the Director to appoint an officer for the post of Curator for the newly established botanic station at Kotu in Gambia. Thiselton-Dyer recommended Walter Haydon, a former Kew member of staff. Haydon took up the post and set about developing the station, planting economically viable crops. Within a few years, coffee, kola, cotton, jute, indigo, couscous, rubber and various fruits were all successfully growing at the station. The house in this photograph was built for the Curator in 1898, so that he could always be on site, in a location that commanded 'a view of all the ground under cultivation'.

LEFT

In his Annual Report of 1898, Hayden writes of how new nursery beds were established near the Curator's House and planted up with seedlings that he had brought back in Wardian cases from Kew. Shades made of oil palm fronds were set up over the young plants to protect them from the fierce sun. The Wardian cases were painted and sent back to Kew the following year, containing living plants.

ABOVE

Grahamstown Botanical Gardens (now Makana Botanical Gardens) were created in 1853 and
are thought to be the second oldest botanic gardens in South Africa. The Gardens supplied
plants and seeds, such as fruit trees, to the whole of the Cape, as well as exchanging seeds
with Kew. This is the Fordyce Conservatory, which was built in the 1850s to commemorate
the death of Colonel Fordyce, whose coat of arms can be seen above the entrance.

LEFT

The cannonball tree, *Couroupita guianensis*, is native to the southern Caribbean and tropical northern South America; this particular specimen was photographed at the Botanical Gardens in Georgetown. Related to the Brazil nut tree, it is often grown for its spectacular, sweet-smelling orange or crimson flowers, which cluster together in large arrangements. The name originates from the large, round, brown fruits, which can measure up to 25cm (10in) in diameter and contain around 250 seeds each. In contrast to the flowers, the fruit has a putrid odour. The plant is often seen as a botanical oddity, and would have seemed quite alien to visiting Europeans.

LEFT

The Botanical Gardens in Georgetown, the capital of Guyana (then British Guiana), were established in 1878 after Mr H. Prestoe, a botanist from Trinidad, visited the city. He laid out plans for a garden on part of an abandoned sugar plantation and under his supervision John Frederick Waby from the Royal Botanic Gardens in Trinidad set to work realizing those plans, bringing with him plants that he had propagated at the Brickdam Observatory. He dedicated the next 35 years of his life to the Gardens.

Lining the road shown here are orinogue trees (*Erythrina glauca*), also known as the coral tree on account of their flame-coloured flowers. The indigenous trees were considered to be the best of their kind and many cuttings were made from them.

RIGHT

A view across a lake in the Botanical Gardens in Georgetown. The lakes form an attractive feature and were created during early landscaping, as a consequence of draining marshland.

Plant-hunting for Kew

Nineteenth-century plant collectors travelled in areas little known to Westerners and worked in often difficult conditions without the modern conveniences we take for granted today. Joseph Hooker embarked on his travels during the mid 19th century, during photography's early years when equipment was bulky, burdensome, and easily damaged, so he chose to produce extensive drawings documenting the culture and landscape that he encountered. However, photographs were beginning to be an important tool, and during his travels to the United States Hooker purchased photographs of the huge trees that he observed. By the early 20th century photographic equipment was much more portable, and plant-hunters such as Ernest Wilson could record every aspect of their travels, including their campsites and local inhabitants as well as the plants they found.

While some plant-collectors used a network of contacts and an entourage of assistants on their travels, taking such luxuries as china and silver cutlery with them, many more travelled light, using temporary, sometimes makeshift shelters, employing local guides and living in harsh conditions. All equipment for botanising had to be carried, including the vasculum for carrying cuttings, plant presses, Wardian cases for transporting live plants, microscopes, reference books and paper for sketching and blotting, as well as more everyday kit such as clothing and food. Plant specimens were vulnerable to insect and environmental damage, and live specimens often died on the long journey back.

Extremes of heat and cold from the tropics to the tundras were explored as the Victorian craze for exotic plants increased, but the individuals who travelled across the globe to collect, catalogue and convey new species were not always employed in the name of science. Some, such as Richard Spruce, were commissioned by the government to collect plants for commercial propagation within the Empire, while others did not have a primary role as collectors; they worked ostensibly in other areas, as missionaries, soldiers, sailors, and government officials. Many, including Joseph Hooker, made use of their scientific education and found employment as surgeons on ships or attached to army regiments. Later in his career, Hooker had a network of amateur collectors whom he called upon to augment Kew's collections of dried and living specimens.

Others were engaged by commercial nurseries to collect specimens that would ultimately be sold as garden exotics. Ernest Wilson, for example, began his career travelling vast distances in lands only recently opened up to the West. With Thiselton-Dyer's endorsement, Wilson was sponsored by James Veitch on an expedition to China, where he successfully discovered specimens that were eventually sold at Veitch's nurseries in England. He is perhaps best known for his intrepid search for the handkerchief tree, or dove tree (*Davidia involucrata*, named for Père David, the French missionary and naturalist who first described

it), a rare tree famous for its characteristic white bracts. With a hand-drawn map and a local guide, Wilson tracked down the tree, only to find that all that remained of it was a stump and a newly built wooden house nearby. Some years later he did finally locate a living example of this extraordinary tree, and at long last was able to dispatch seeds to England.

LEFT

This photograph of *Davidia involucrata*, known as the handkerchief or dove tree, was taken in June 1907 by Ernest Wilson near Hsing-shan Hsien, West Hupeh, at an altitude of 1646m (5400ft). Some of the bracts that give the tree its common name can still be seen in the lower branches; they are particularly striking during the month of May, when the tree is in full flower.

ABOVE

Charles Darwin established his career as a naturalist with
an expedition to South America on board HMS *Beagle*. It
was this voyage, along with the plant, animal and geological
specimens he collected, that helped Darwin to formulate his
theories on species mutation and evolution. After Darwin's
return to England the plant specimens were passed to Joseph
Hooker at Kew, where they now reside in the Herbarium.
Hooker first met Darwin in 1839, before embarking on
his own first expedition, on board HMS *Erebus*. A long
correspondence began and Hooker and Darwin shared a
close relationship, both professionally and personally. Hooker
was a key supporter of Darwin, challenging and examining
his theories, as well as providing many seeds from Kew for
his experiments. Darwin wrote of this photograph that he
liked it very much better than other photographs of himself.

Marianne North generally travelled unaccompanied, an extraordinary feat for a Victorian lady, only occasionally using letters of introduction to enable her to stay with the associates of those she met on her travels. Between 1871 and 1879, she visited Canada, the United States, Jamaica, Brazil, Japan, Sarawak, Singapore, Java, Sri Lanka and India. In 1880, Marianne met Charles Darwin, whom she regarded as 'the greatest man living, the most truthful as well as the most unselfish and modest'. On his suggestion, she set off on a further voyage, this time encompassing Australia and New Zealand. In 1882 she visited Africa, the final continent left unrepresented in her work; this photograph shows her sketching the local flora in Grahamstown, South Africa. In 1885 she made a final voyage to South America.

ABOVE

Joseph Hooker had travelled to the Antarctic and the Himalayas before taking up his post at Kew in 1855, but did not have the opportunity for plant-collecting expeditions again until the 1870s. In 1877, along with his old family friend Asa Gray, the eminent American botanist, Hooker was invited by the United States Geological and Geographical Survey to join an expedition to survey the Rocky Mountains. Hooker took the opportunity to meet up with his friend and also to spend time plant-collecting in Colorado, Utah and California, covering 12,875km (8000 miles) in just 10 weeks. In this photograph, taken in the Rockies in Colorado at 2743m (9000ft), Asa Gray is sitting on the ground at the front, with Hooker seated to his right. They are surrounded by plant specimens and Gray is holding a plant press.

ABOVE

During his expedition to the western United States, Joseph Hooker met John Muir, a Scottish-born naturalist best known for his campaign to preserve the American wilderness. In 1882, Muir wrote to Hooker, 'The memories of our camp among the firs and pines and spruce of Shasta will always be bright and joyful. How glad I should be . . . if you and Gray would pair again and come once more to the woods and plains of the Pacific'. The purpose of the letter was to enlist Hooker's support of a Congressional bill to preserve 'a large section of Sequoia forests of the Sierra on the Kaweah and Tule rivers', beautiful landscapes such as the one illustrated here. Muir clearly had much respect and confidence in Joseph's influence, and was 'sure that a word from you on the importance of the bill would carry a grand pushing power and go far towards insuring the success of the effort'.

ABOVE

This *Quercus lobata* was given the name 'The Hooker Oak' by Annie Bidwell, pioneer and social campaigner, an influential woman whose friends included the civil rights activist Susan B. Anthony and Ulysses S. Grant, US President 1869–1877. Hooker saw the oak which grew on the Bidwells' land in Chico, California during a visit to the area in 1877, and was said to have judged it to be the "largest live-oak in the known world". The tree became emblematic to the city, growing in fame until the Bidwells allegedly had to put up signs requesting that people do not 'mutilate this noble oak'. It even appeared as part of Sherwood Forest in Warner Brothers' 1937 film *Robin Hood and his Merry Men*, starring Errol Flynn. On Annie's death, the land was gifted to the city and the oak was awarded the status of a California State Monument. In 1977 it was destroyed during a storm.

ABOVE

The colossal scale of the giant redwoods made them a fascinating subject. Here a group of people join hands to convey the massive breadth of one of them; this particular tree, *Sequoia sempervirens*, was recorded as measuring 18m (60ft) in circumference. Native to western North America, primarily California, *S. sempervirens* is one of the largest trees on the planet and can grow to heights of 110m (360ft), as this one did.

LEFT

Here, a pioneer cabin has been built into the base of a *Sequoiadendron giganteum* (giant sequoia, or giant redwood). Native to California, it is the only living species in the genus. Hooker purchased this photograph, probably during his expedition to the United States. It shows the resourcefulness of the settlers, who could turn a naturally formed cavity in the roots of a tree into a shelter, as well as illustrating the massive circumference of the trunk.

ABOVE

Shown in an image from Henry Ridley's collection is a camp
on Pulau Lalang, a small island off the coast of Malaysia.
In the earlier days of plant hunting it was not unusual for
items such as silver cutlery, writing desks and beds to be
taken on well-funded expeditions. Here a more practical
approach can be seen, as necessitated by the region
being explored and possibly also by lack of funding.

RIGHT

This photograph of Alexander Wollaston, doctor, explorer and
naturalist, is from an album illustrating the zoological and
botanical expedition Wollaston led to the Snow Mountains
of Dutch New Guinea in 1912–13. The album was given to
Henry Ridley by C. Boden Kloss, the expedition's naturalist,
in recognition of the help he gave to the expedition.

Ernest Wilson lodged at these buildings in Hubei Province in central China while on his second expedition for the Arnold Arboretum (1909–11). Where possible, plant-hunters would stay at local inns or with contacts – who, in the case of someone well-connected like Joseph Hooker or Marianne North, could offer luxurious accommodation. However, when collecting in uninhabited or unknown areas, camping would become a necessity and many dangers such as wild animals, robbery and extremes of temperature were encountered.

Here, John Davenport Snowden and his wife stand outside their tent at a camp near Kampala, Uganda, in 1916. Snowden began work in Uganda in 1911, when he became Assistant Agricultural Officer. He remained in the country for the next 20 years and frequently made expeditions to plantations to give advice on cultivation, collecting specimens as he travelled. In the earlier years, these journeys were made on foot or bicycle, with 20–30 porters carrying equipment and food. Snowden is remembered for his extensive botanical exploration of Uganda. He sent many specimens back to Kew, including grasses and the red-hot poker *Kniphofia thompsonii* var. *snowdenii*, named after him.

ABOVE

When Henry Ridley took over the directorship of the Singapore Botanic Gardens, there were
many overgrown jungle areas and he was tasked with making a preliminary forest survey.
Ridley is holding a machete for cutting his way through the undergrowth, while his assistant
is carrying a vasculum for any interesting specimens that they might come upon.

While he was Director of Kew (1922–41), Arthur Hill retained the passion for travel that he had developed in the preceding years. In 1903 he participated in an expedition to Peru and Bolivia, and the flora that he encountered in the Andes made such an impression on him that he worked on Andean plants throughout his professional career. As Director, Hill travelled more than any of his predecessors, building on Kew's international links. Back at Kew, he took a keen interest in the daily running of the Gardens, using his extensive knowledge of horticulture to develop the planting and making daily inspections.

This photograph of Hill was taken while he was on the Bolivian expedition. Although he is almost unrecognizable, his vasculum can just be discerned beneath his poncho.

ABOVE

Mrs Snowden, the wife of John Davenport Snowden, is seen here being carried in a monowheel car in Kampala, Uganda.

RIGHT

A keen horseman, Arthur Hill used to take a ride every morning but sadly met his death in 1941 when he fell from his horse on the Mid Surrey Golf Course, in the Old Deer Park, Richmond. The directorship of Kew then passed to the Deputy Director, Geoffrey Evans.

LEFT

This boat, built almost completely of cypress wood, is characteristic of houseboats used in China in the 19th and early 20th centuries and is similar to the one used by Wilson while travelling along China's waterways, including his voyage along the Yangtze River, then known as Chang Jiang. He named his first boat Ellena, after his wife.

LEFT

Here, Henry Ridley is standing by
a houseboat at Kuala Tembeling in
Malaysia, 1911. While Director of
Singapore Botanic Gardens, Ridley
travelled extensively throughout the
Malay Peninsula, recording the flora
and collecting specimens. He sent
large numbers of specimens back to
Kew, as well as making collections
for his own herbarium in Singapore.

RIGHT

As more sophisticated means of transport developed,
botanical exploration became easier. No longer did it take
months or even years of travel to reach certain regions
and transporting living material became easier too. This
photograph shows a young Reginald Rose-Innes, who
was to become an eminent grassland ecologist.

RIGHT AND LEFT

The photograph on the right shows Reginald Rose-Innes
having breakfast in the desert with 'Oscar', the car, behind,
while that on the left shows his expedition party beside
the campfire. Life in the field was often extremely hard and
even in more modern times, supplies could be difficult to
obtain. On a later expedition in the Namibian desert, Rose-
Innes was forced to survive on whatever he could catch or
forage. Some botanists, however, did manage to carry a
few home comforts with them. Among the papers of the
plant hunter Frank Kingdon-Ward, a bill from Fortnum &
Mason's export department can be found, listing Heinz baked
beans, HP sauce and tins of Cadbury's Mexican chocolate.

This group photograph of 'Kewites and wives', taken in Kampala in 1923, illustrates how common it was for botanists working in the field to take their family with them. John Davenport Snowden, seated second right with his wife (centre), had begun his career as a gardener at Kew in 1909, and went on to become Senior District Agricultural Officer in Uganda, where this photograph was taken. Arthur Marshall (back row, far right) was the 'pony boy' in the Gardens, but after attending lectures he obtained the Kew Certificate, and was elected honorary member of the Ugandan Branch; his wife is seated in front of him. The third woman, Dorothy Halkerston, sits in front of her husband, Donald Halkerston, chair of the Ugandan Branch of the Kew Guild.

Frank Kingdon-Ward took part in more than 20 expeditions over 50 years, exploring north-west China, Tibet, Burma and north-east India. In 1924, he collected the first specimen of *Primula florindae*, the giant cowslip, which he named after his first wife, Florinda. Here he is seen with Jean (née Macklin), his second wife. *Lilium mackliniae*, which they discovered together in Manipur, is named after her.

Joseph Rock (1884–1962), a Viennese-born naturalist, emigrated to Hawaii via the United States in his early twenties, and went on to become an authority on the island's flora. Despite a relatively disadvantaged start to life and a dislike of formal education, Rock, a self-taught linguist who was fluent in Hungarian, English, Latin, French, Italian, Greek, Chinese, Arabic and Sanskrit in addition to his native German, published 40 botanical works over a 10-year period. Even so, he felt the need to invent a university career to gain the approval of his peers. His first journey was to Burma and Assam in 1920 to search for the chaulmoogra tree, the source of a treatment for leprosy. From 1922 to 1949, he travelled through south-west China studying the flora, peoples, culture and languages of the region, producing articles for the *National Geographic*. Here he is dressed in traditional Tibetan attire.

ABOVE

William Turrill was Keeper of the Herbarium
and Library 1946–57. His particular botanical
interests were the flora of the Balkans and
phytogeography – the geographic distribution
of plants. Here he can be seen botanising
aquatic plants with his vasculum slung over
his shoulder. The vasculum is an important tool
for botanists collecting in the field; often made
of metal and of a cylindrical shape, it acts as
a container to preserve freshly picked plants.
Popular interest in naturalism, and in particular
botany, during the early part of the 19th century
was such that vascula were mass-produced.

John Hutchinson began his career at Kew
as a student gardener in 1904, but his
proficiency in taxonomy (the classification
of plants) and his drawing skills resulted in
his transfer to the Herbarium just one year
later. After working with both the Indian and
Tropical African collections and writing and
illustrating many botanical books, he was
appointed Keeper of the Museums of Botany
at Kew in 1936, a post he retained until his
retirement in 1948. Here he can be seen
on expedition in Northern Transvaal in 1930,
using his plant-press as a makeshift seat.
The oldest dried plant at Kew dates back to
around 1700, and such specimens are vital to
botanists when identifying species. Specimens
have to be thoroughly dried to prevent
discoloration and fermentation, so plant-
presses are indispensable field equipment.

LEFT

The Wardian case was a portable airtight
greenhouse developed by Nathaniel Bagshaw
Ward (1791–1868). As he lived in the docklands
area of London, Ward's interest in amateur
botany was thwarted by the polluted, sooty
air that killed everything he tried to grow.
After turning his interest to entomology, he
noticed that hawk moth chrysalises left in
a glass jar flourished, as did fern seedlings,
protected from the smoky environment.
The Wardian case revolutionized botany
in the 19th century, allowing live plants
to be transported across the globe.

ABOVE

Frank Kingdon-Ward's plant-hunting career began when he
joined an American zoological expedition to China in 1909,
aged 24. From then on, collecting became his profession
and he made a number of expeditions to Asia, collecting
extensively, including many new species of rhododendron, as
his predecessor Joseph Hooker had done in the 1850s. However,
he is probably best known for collecting the first viable seeds
of *Meconopsis betonicifolia*, the Himalayan blue poppy.

After his first marriage broke down, Kingdon-Ward married
Jean Macklin, who was 36 years his junior. Jean shared his passion
for exploration and travelling, and often accompanied him on his
plant-hunting expeditions. These two images of river crossings
were taken on the Kingdon-Wards' expedition to the Lohit Valley,
Assam in 1950; one of the largest recorded earthquakes had
struck, causing great devastation and destroying the bridge over
the Lohit river. Jean had fallen ill and had to be carried for large
parts of the journey out of the valley. In the right-hand image, she
can be seen in the foreground, being borne across the river.

LEFT

Meconopsis betonicifolia,
the Himalayan blue
poppy, photographed
by Kingdon-Ward.

Here Jean Kingdon-Ward is bidding 'a nostalgic farewell' to the mountains in northern Burma, 1953. On this plant-hunting expedition, the Kingdon-Wards collected many plants and covered 1126km (700 miles) on foot. Frank was 68 by this time and this expedition was to be one of his last.

Carrying some freshly collected specimens on the Burmese expedition, Jean is shown talking to local people, Burma 1953. Indigenous knowledge of plants and their uses, and also of locations where certain specimens might grow, was of great importance to plant hunters.

ABOVE

At the age of 17, Ernest Henry Wilson began working at Birmingham Botanical Gardens as a gardener. Once his working day was over, he studied botany at Birmingham Technical School, gaining first class and a Queen's Prize in the advanced level examination in June 1896. The following year, Wilson began work as a gardener at Kew while studying at the Royal Horticultural Society. Here he is seen (back row, second from right) with his Kew colleagues. In 1898, Wilson began a full-time course in botany at the Royal College of Science, with the aim of becoming a teacher.

During the 1880s, Augustine Henry, a British Medical Officer working in China, sent over 2500 specimens to Kew. Five hundred of his specimens were from species previously unknown in the West, and he recommended in correspondence with Sir William Thiselton-Dyer that the institution send a collector to the region. James Veitch & Sons at Chelsea were also keen to dispatch a collector to China, and approached Thiselton-Dyer to suggest a talented individual for the job. He could think of no one better than Wilson. Thus began Wilson's long connection with the Veitchs, and it was his journeys through China that earned him the epithet 'Chinese' Wilson. He set off on the first of many tours to the region in 1899.

ABOVE

In 1906, Wilson again travelled to China, but this time for the Arnold Arboretum at Harvard University, Boston, where he eventually became Keeper in 1927. Under its sponsorship, he also made expeditions to Japan, and later to India, Africa, Central America and Australasia. Here, a figure resembling Wilson is dwarfed by a massive *Eucalyptus obliqua* in the Kuitpo Government Forest in South Australia. In his photographs, he often used the device of placing a man beside the specimen to illustrate scale.

RIGHT

During his first expedition for the Arnold Arboretum, between 1906 and 1909, Wilson took two cameras, a large-format Sanderson, which used glass plates, and a small Kodak which used recently invented roll-film, which was of a much poorer quality. The images he made during this expedition show his apparently innate aptitude for photography and composition. This photograph, taken north-east of Kangding in July 1908, is of the peaks of the Ta-p'ao-shan Range, which reach more than 6400m (21,000ft).

LEFT

The horizontal struts attached to this *Rhus vernicifera*, or varnish tree, allow workers gathering the milk-like and highly caustic sap to scale the tree without making contact with its trunk. This sap was prized for its use in the manufacture of lacquerware but is very toxic, containing a corrosive compound called urushiol, an oil that in its liquid form can cause acute allergic reactions and even as a vapour is highly noxious.

ABOVE

This field of *Platycodon grandiflorum*, or balloon flower, cultivated for its medicinal properties, is in Chin-tang Hsien, Sichuan Province. *Platycodon* was applied as an astringent and was also used as a sedative, pain-killer, digestive aid and expellant of intestinal parasites.

RIGHT

Wilson photographed these cones of *Keteleeria davidiana*, a tree native to Taiwan and south-east China, in a street in Pa-tung Hsien (Badong), Hubei Province, in 1910. The cones are illustrated in fine detail, framed against a wall-painting and with the figure of a man in the background. The image was taken during Wilson's second trip to China for the Arnold Arboretum. Carrying the exposed plates with him, he would only process the negatives, develop the prints, and finally see the images when he returned home.

Wilson photographed this *Styphnolobium japonicum* (then called *Sophora japonica*), or Chinese scholar tree, in July 1910. More commonly known in the West as the pagoda tree, it was seen by Wilson in a street in Chengdu in Sichuan Province – one of China's oldest cities, and formerly an imperial capital.

ABOVE

This *Gleditsia macracantha* was photographed by Wilson at Yichang in Hubei Province, 19 March 1908; the boards are votive offerings to the healing spirit which was believed to inhabit the tree. The alkaloid stenocarpine (a local anaesthetic) can be extracted from its leaves and twigs.

RIGHT

Eucommia ulmoides, is commonly known in China as the Tu-Chung, and was cultivated in the hills of central and western regions for its bark, which was highly valued for its medicinal properties as a tonic. This man is carrying a load of the bark through the mountainous region of Sichuan.

Wilson's view of the Chentu Plain shows
examples of cypress trees, bamboo and
Pterocarya stenoptera. The building is described
by him as a 'typical farm house', and the figures
in the photograph are ploughing the land.

PLANT-HUNTING
FOR KEW

ABOVE

For many hundreds of years Tachien-lu, now known as
Kangding – or, to the Tibetans, as Dartsedo – was a major
trading centre inhabited by a diverse populace of Chinese
and Tibetan communities, where commodities such as
musk, precious metals, animal skins and Tibetan wool
were exchanged for tea bricks and tobacco. The town,
which lies at an altitude of almost 1500m (4800ft), sits
beneath tall snow-capped mountains and was nearly
destroyed in 1794 by a landslide set off by an earthquake.
Wilson referred to it as a 'small and filthy place'.

RIGHT

Wilson estimated that the
load borne by this man
weighed about 121kg
(267lb). The bowls are
made from the wood of
the *Pinus massoniana*,
Chinese red pine or horsetail
pine, native to central
and southern China.

LEFT AND ABOVE

Having studied for a masters' degree in South Africa, Reginald Rose-Innes continued his education in the United States, where he took the opportunity to travel extensively, photographing his trips. In the 1950s, he returned to Africa to take up a research post at what was to become the University of Ghana. Rose-Innes frequently made expeditions to research grassland ecology, and collected many grasses that he sent back to Kew. He later worked for the Food and Agricultural Organization under the United Nations and then the Ministry of Overseas Surveys in the UK. Even after his retirement, Rose-Innes' sense of adventure was prevalent and he set a British record when he became the oldest person to fly tandem on a paraglider at the age of 91.

These photographs show the difficult terrains in which plant hunters and botanists had to work; mountains, deserts and jungles had to be traversed without modern-day equipment and maps. Here Rose-Innes is scaling a mountain and we can see specimens being collected. Occasionally, the plant-hunters were the first Westerners to visit certain locations and they were clearly impressed by the scenery, as well as the botanical specimens. In the photograph to the left, Rose-Innes admires a view he has come across.

Visiting Kew

During the 19th century the concept of the public park and pleasure garden became popular, with many being developed to offer people areas in which to spend their leisure time – in itself a relatively new luxury for the working classes, with public bank holidays being introduced by an Act of Parliament in 1871. Such places provided health and educational benefits and a distraction from the allure of the prevalent gin palaces.

As a result, there was constant pressure on William Hooker and later Joseph and his successors to increase public opening hours to the Gardens and to provide public facilities. When Kew was part of the royal estate the public had been admitted on certain days and for limited periods of time. When the pleasure gardens (later to become the Arboretum) came under William's control in 1845, they were open to the general public from 1pm on Thursdays and Sundays only, although the small botanic garden was open every afternoon except Sundays. As the working classes had

only one or two days' holiday a year it was hard for these visitors to gain access, so gradually, under great pressure from the public and the press, opening hours were extended.

Having defended Kew's position as a scientific institution and secured its future in a battle with Acton Smee Ayrton, Financial Secretary to the Treasury, in the early 1870s, Joseph Hooker was keen to protect the Gardens' botanical standing and to keep out 'pleasure or recreational seekers . . . whose motives are rude rompings and games'. He withstood pressure from groups such as The Kew Gardens Public Rights Defence Association to open in the mornings and to remove the boundary wall on Kew Road, although he conceded to opening at 10am on bank holidays. Despite this resistance, Joseph did much to develop the experience for those he deemed suitable. He altered the landscape of the Gardens, introducing many new walkways, particularly in the Arboretum, making it easier to promenade, and developed vistas and avenues around

the Pagoda, including the Holly Walk.

Kew also had many follies and buildings remaining from its royal life, such as the Ruined Arch and Queen Charlotte's Cottage, which made the Gardens attractive to visitors. One major facility that was lacking was any kind of restaurant; this was a concession to the public that Joseph never allowed. He vehemently denied Marianne North's request for tea and coffee to be served in her Gallery and it was not until Thiselton-Dyer became Director that a refreshment pavilion was opened between the Gallery and the Temperate House in 1888.

With improvements to public transport and greater leisure time, visitor numbers steadily increased, eventually resulting in extended opening hours. Since 1921 the Gardens have opened daily, morning and afternoon, apart from on Christmas Day, welcoming visitors and presenting new attractions to encourage the next generation of Kew enthusiasts.

ABOVE

Sir William Chambers' Orangery, built in 1761 in the classical style and constructed from brick and stucco, is his only remaining plant house in the Gardens today. It was never truly a practical building for cultivating citrus fruits; the windows were not large enough to allow adequate levels of light for the plants to thrive. When William Hooker took over the running of the Gardens he installed glass doors to increase the light levels, and for a time the building accommodated plants too large for the other plant houses. In 1863 it became Museum No. 3, and displayed Kew's wood collections.

38921 Kew Pier,

ABOVE

Travel by river was a popular way of reaching Kew and Richmond for many centuries. The roads were generally poor and often frequented by highwaymen, and most of the Thames bridges imposed a toll. Steam boats were introduced in 1816. Initially they went straight to Richmond without stopping at Kew, but eventually a stop at Kew Pier was added. Kew Bridge railway station opened in 1853 and Kew Gardens in 1869. Connecting Kew with central London had a huge impact on visitor numbers to the Gardens, as accessibility improved. In 1873 the tolls on Kew Bridge were abolished and again visitor numbers increased, rising from 231,010 in 1852, to 699,426 in 1874.

ABOVE

From 1883 to 1912, horse-drawn trolley-buses, or trackless trams, ran to Kew Bridge
from the Orange Tree public house near Richmond Station on the Kew Road. This image
shows a trolley-bus on the Kew Road, just outside one of the entrances to the Gardens.
Once motorized vehicles were introduced, these trolley-buses fell into disuse.

THE VICTORIA GATES, KEW GARDENS.

ABOVE

Designed by William Nesfield, the Queen's Gate was built in 1868 to provide a new entrance for visitors arriving by train via the new branch line of the London and South West Railway. However, when Kew Gardens station was eventually opened, it was sited further north, prompting the gates to be moved to their current location. Renamed Victoria Gate, they were opened on 27 May 1889. The Portland stone pillars are carved with the crown and 'VR' for 'Victoria Regina' within roundels.

LEFT

The lion that surmounts this gate formerly adorned one of George IV's lodges at the original entrance on Kew Green. When this lodge was demolished, the sculpture was moved to a different site on the Kew Road, now known as Lion Gate. Designed by Thomas Hardewicke, the lion is made from a semi-vitreous ceramic material known as coade stone, that mimics stone sculpture. The building in the photograph, Lion Gate Lodge, was originally built for use as staff accommodation during the late 19th century, and has the Dutch gables, tall chimneys and red brickwork which are typical of Victorian Tudor Revival. The gate is also sometimes called the Pagoda Gate on account of its proximity to the Pagoda.

LEFT

The turnstiles were established when a charge was first introduced in 1916, with visitors paying one penny. The Gardens were open to the public on Mondays, Wednesdays, Thursdays and Saturdays; Tuesdays and Fridays were reserved for students who paid six pence for the benefit of having the Gardens to themselves.

RIGHT

Kew's oldest entrance, the main gate on Kew Green, was established in 1825 while the Gardens were still in royal ownership in order to divide their domains from the intrusion of 'vulgar curiosity'. The original gate was flanked by two lodges, upon which sat stone statues depicting a lion and a unicorn. When William Hooker assumed his role as Director, he thought that the now public gardens deserved a more imposing entrance. The gates that currently stand at the main entrance were designed by Decimus Burton, and were opened for the first time in 1846. The pillars are carved from Portland stone; their fruit and floral reliefs, and the royal coat of arms on the gates, befitted the Gardens' status as an emerging botanical institution.

THE QUEEN'S COTTAGE, KEW.

ABOVE

Queen Charlotte's Cottage was situated in what was originally the New Menagerie, where, from 1792, exotic animals such as kangaroos were kept. It is unknown what the original purpose of the building was and exactly when it was built, but it is most likely to originate from the mid-18th century, when such rustic cottages were fashionable follies. Although the royal family used the secluded cottage for picnics, ornate decorations and furniture were added. In 1898 Queen Victoria donated the cottage and its lands to Kew. The cottage and the surrounding bluebell woods are still popular visitor attractions today, allowing a glimpse of a royal hideaway.

RIGHT

In the 18th century, William Chambers designed a number of follies in the Gardens for the royal family, of which several are still standing and form part of the Gardens' attractions. The Ruined Arch is one such folly, built by Chambers in 1759. However, the Romanesque structure also originally had a practical purpose, forming a bridge over a path for grazing animals to be led into the Gardens' pastures. The Arch had to be rebuilt in 1932 and still stands over the path that runs alongside the wall bordering Kew Road. It has recently been discovered that the Arch, designed to look ruined, contains genuine Graeco-Roman stone work.

KEW GARDENS & PALACE.

ABOVE

Kew Palace is the oldest building in the Gardens, constructed in 1631 for a merchant, Samuel Fortrey. About
100 years later, it was leased by Queen Caroline, and was subsequently bought by George III. It was used as
a country retreat for the royal family up until 1898, when it was opened to the public. The Palace played an
essential role in the history of Kew, as it was the royal family's residency here that led to the establishment of the
botanic garden that formed the foundations of the present Gardens. Today, the public can still visit the Palace.

RIGHT

In 1912 the Rock Garden was rebuilt. Logs and tree stumps that had been used to masquerade as rocks because of the lack of available stone were disposed of and the material from demolished buildings was hidden from sight. With the expansion of the Bog Garden, the Dripping Well shown here was removed and a waterfall was added to the garden.

LEFT AND ABOVE

To address the demands of alpine enthusiasts after 3000 alpine plants were left to Kew, a large rock garden was designed by William Thiselton-Dyer. A site between the T-Range and the Herbaceous Ground was chosen and the design was based around a 157m (514ft) long winding path, intended to emulate the dry bed of a stream. The garden opened to the public in 1882, forming a new principal attraction. Wild flowers and plants were used where possible, although this was not always appreciated by the Gardens' visitors, who were reported in the horticultural press to have complained that 'there seems to be too much space given over to weeds and wild flowers'.

LEFT

The Japan-British Exhibition of 1910, held at Shepherds Bush, consisted of 100 buildings covering an area of 40 hectares (100 acres) and attracted 8 million visitors. The buildings were painted white, giving rise to the name 'White City', which is still used to describe that area of London. When it closed, the Chokushi-Mon (Gateway of the Imperial Messenger), better known as the Japanese Gateway, was presented to the Gardens as a gift. The structure is a four-fifths-size model of the Karamon of Nishi Hongan-ji in Kyoto, Japan's ancient imperial capital.

LEFT

The Titan arum, *Amorphophallus titanum*, is known as the corpse flower in its native Indonesia because of the rancid smell, described in *Curtis's Botanical Magazine* as 'a mixture of rotten fish and burnt sugar', which it emits as it flowers. It caused a sensation when it first bloomed at Kew in June 1889; the odour attracted 'many blue-bottle flies', and visitors were greatly disturbed by the smell. The artist Matilda Smith, who recorded this first flowering for the *Botanical Magazine*, endured many hours painting it and consequently felt ill. The flower, or more correctly inflorescence, can grow to more than 2.5m (8¼ft) and is surrounded by a single purple leaf. These photographs were taken over a four-day period during a later blooming in 1901.

Adjacent to the Woodland Glade at the south end of the Gardens is the Waterlily Pond, one of Sir William Thiselton-Dyer's additions. The pool was heated by condensed steam from the local water supply, making it possible to raise half-hardy aquatic plants. Some of the waterlilies in this photograph from about 1900 were supplied by the French nurseryman Joseph Bory Latour-Marliac. One of the first growers to successfully hybridize waterlilies, Marliac is probably best known for his yellow-flowered cultivar *Nymphaea 'Marliacea Chromatella'*, which he sent to Kew in 1887. He is also renowned for contributing many of the waterlilies in Monet's garden at Giverny.

THE ROSE PERGOLA NEAR THE ROCK GARDEN.
KEW GARDENS.

ABOVE

Kew's first Rose Pergola, situated between the Rock Garden and Herbaceous Ground, was constructed in 1901 to provide a pleasantly fragranced and shaded pathway. In 1959, to mark the Gardens' bicentenary, the existing Rose Pergola was erected above the main path through the Order Beds, a collection of plants arranged by family.

Bluebells are emblematic of Britain's woodland habitat, and 30–50 per cent of the world's population can be found in the UK. When Queen Charlotte's Cottage was presented to the Gardens by Queen Victoria, she stipulated that the surrounding land be kept in an uncultivated state. In April and May each year this area is blanketed with bluebells, and although some changes have been made, the Queen's wishes have largely been followed.

LEFT

Daffodils have a special place in British culture; celebrated in art and poetry, associated with the arrival of spring, they are probably the most popular garden flowers. During the 19th century, at Kew and across London, the first weekend in April was celebrated as 'Daffodil Sunday', when people would pick flowers from their garden to give to the sick in local hospitals. Today, a yellow carpet of more than 100,000 daffodils surrounds Kew's Broadwalk from February to May.

LEFT

During the 19th century, strict regulations were in place regarding visitors to the Gardens. They were not allowed to bring food; they had to be decently attired; and smoking, 'play' and prams were forbidden. Joseph Hooker was vehemently opposed to having refreshments in the Gardens and it was not until after his retirement that the first refreshment pavilion opened in 1888, situated between the Temperate House and the Marianne North Gallery. The pavilion served tea and cold collations when it first opened. In 1913 the pavilion was burnt down by members of the women's suffrage movement as part of their campaign. They also attacked the orchid houses, smashing some of the glass and destroying plants, resulting in headlines such as 'Mad women raid Kew Gardens' (*Daily Express*). Near left, visitors sit outside the first pavilion's replacement, which was opened in 1920.

ABOVE

Celia André (centre) was born in Windsor, moving to Richmond while still a child. Divorced in 1926, with two small children, she had to take up employment and found work at Kew as a waitress. She was supplied with a uniform which included shoes with heels 10cm (4in) high and was given a set number of tables to work. She relied on tips, which were often very generous, to supplement her low wage. Customers most commonly ordered a set tea, which consisted of a pot of tea with bread and jam and a selection of fancy cakes. Although she remarried in 1929, she kept her job into the early 1930s, when she had her third child. Work was hard, but she enjoyed her life at Kew and spoke fondly of the camaraderie of the other waitresses and the sharing of cakes left by customers.

ABOVE

This cartoon was produced in 1878 as part of the ongoing debate about whether the general public should be allowed into the Gardens in the morning. Only 'respectable individuals' – mostly botanists or botanical artists – were allowed in the Gardens before 1pm and then only with the Director's permission. The Kew Gardens Public Rights Defence Association was established to campaign for earlier public opening hours and gradually visiting times were extended. The author of the piece that accompanied this cartoon, who disguised himself as a German botanist in order to gain entry, reported seeing 'favoured young ladies' on 'snug seats, reading novels', 'gentlemen who may have been eminent botanists, but who were most certainly fast asleep in garden chairs' and 'other gentlemen . . . engaged in testing the effects of cigar smoke on open-air evergreens'.

ABOVE

This stereograph of the interior of one of the T-Range glasshouses shows a sign requesting visitors to keep to the right and to refrain from touching the plants. Stereographs were extremely popular from the 1850s until the early 20th century and were used to illustrate key visitor attractions. This image, one of two, depicting left and right eye images of the same scene would have been viewed along with the left eye image, through a stereoscope and appear to the viewer to be a single three-dimensional image.

ABOVE

William Dallimore joined Kew as a student gardener in 1891, eventually becoming Keeper of the Museums of Economic Botany. Describing a bank holiday in the 1890s, he wrote that the visitors enjoyed themselves 'seriously enough as long as they were within the Gardens, but . . . as the Gardens were cleared, they remained on Kew Green for two or three hours and a large kiss-in-the-ring was formed to which all comers were welcome, and the fun became fast and furious'. Stalls on the Green sold cockles, cakes, tea and lemonade, and fortunes were told for a penny a time. This image shows Kew Green following the August bank holiday celebrations of 1926.

RIGHT

Two aeroplane crashes have been recorded in Kew's history; the first occurred on 16 August 1928, when a single-seater Siskin aircraft came down in flames to the west of the Syon Vista during an aerial display. The damage to the plane was severe, and the wreckage burned for almost 30 minutes. The pilot escaped unharmed, landing by parachute on a roof in Beaumont Avenue near the Lion Gate.

RIGHT

The second crash, which happened almost exactly 10 years later, was not quite as dramatic; this photograph shows an aircraft forced to make an emergency landing near the Palm House on 5 January, 1938. It had been pulling an advertising banner, and onlookers said that the pilot would have made a faultless landing had it not been for the left wing striking a tree during the descent, which caused the craft to spin and land nose first. Fortunately there were no casualties and the plane's dismantling, which took place the following day, drew many spectators.

ABOVE

In 1899, three penguins were presented to Kew by Albert Linney, the head gardener at Government House in the Falkland Islands and a former Kew gardener. At the time there was a great interest in all things relating to the Antarctic and Joseph Hooker provided advice on polar exploration to Captain Robert Falcon Scott. This photograph was taken in 1901, outside Museum No. 1. The man feeding the penguins is Mr Allaway, described as 'the birdman'.

RIGHT

Joey the Stanley Crane was a well-known Kew personality. In 1935 *The Journal of the Kew Guild* described his eventful life, which included losing a toe to a lawn mower, protecting other cranes from an attack by geese, and a love affair with a Demoiselle Crane, having seen off a rival. He met a tragic end, drowning in the Lake on 31 January 1935, when he fell through some thin ice. Local newspapers told of his death, declaring 'Joey of Kew Dead'.

The Kew flagstaffs

For almost 150 years, a flagstaff stood in Kew Gardens. The first, presented in 1861 by a timber merchant named Edward Stamp, based in Canada, was erected on a site formerly occupied by the Temple of Victory. It stood in the Gardens for the next 58 years until in 1913 it was found to be unsafe, having decayed quite considerably, and was taken down.

Almost immediately, as news of the flagstaff's demise spread, a replacement was offered by the Provincial Government of British Columbia. The Assistant Director, Arthur Hill, accepted on Kew's behalf, and the search began for the right tree. Like its predecessor, the new flagpole was produced from the trunk of a Douglas fir, and it was a fine specimen, standing at around 91m (300ft). After felling, the branches were removed and it was reduced to 67m (220ft), then carried by rail and water to Vancouver, where it was finished by specialist axemen. The final pole measured just over 65m (214ft). The flagstaff was shipped to England in 1915 and was towed along the Thames. Its erection was delayed by World War I, and it was not until October 1919 that the flagstaff was finally and smoothly hoisted into place.

The third official flagpole was to be the last; it arrived in the Gardens in 1959, another gift from British Columbia to mark the Province's centenary (1958) and Kew's bicentenary (1959). At the time, it was the tallest wooden flagpole in the world, standing at 68.5m (225ft) and weighing more than 15 tonnes. Cut from a 370-year-old Douglas fir, it was raised into place on 5 November 1959 by 23 Field Squadron of the Royal Engineers and stood for almost 50 years until August 2007. When it too succumbed to decay, the loss of another great tree was considered too high a price, and it was not replaced.

ABOVE

In this photograph of the felled tree taken in 1914, the team responsible for cutting it down illustrate its massive height.

BELOW

The great flagstaff is seen here en route from Vancouver aboard the SS *Merionethshire*, arriving at Tilbury Docks on 29 December 1915.

ABOVE

The flagstaff was towed along the Thames by tug in early 1916 and is seen here arriving at Syon Vista. It was reported in the *Kew Bulletin* that the delay in raising the flagstaff had its advantages: 'The pole as it laid along the ground was a source of pride to Canadians over here, and an object of great interest to home visitors who were able to appreciate its magnificent size and length. It also allowed the wood to be treated thoroughly and conveniently with antiseptic dressings.'

ABOVE

In 1919, the flagpole was erected by means of raising a derrick, a lifting device supported by guy-lines, which stood more than 30m (100ft) high.

ABOVE RIGHT

The great flagstaff is shown here flying the Union Flag; the base was secured by a square steel block.

Kew Behind the Scenes

Kew is a vast organization that employs hundreds of people. Visitors come into contact with only a handful of the staff, as the majority work behind the scenes in disparate roles, from gardeners and scientists to museum curators, artists and administrative staff. Without these staff and their predecessors, Kew would not be what it is today.

Among the more visible roles are those in horticulture, with the staff being responsible for maintenance of the Gardens and curation of the living collections. In the 19th century, about 100 members of staff worked in the horticultural departments under the supervision of the Curator of the Gardens, including about a dozen men employed on the apprenticeship scheme, which eventually became the Kew Diploma. The students worked long hours for little pay, but a Kew apprenticeship held great value and the graduates often moved onto senior positions elsewhere. As well as the apprentices, a foreman and a number of day labourers were employed by each horticultural department, which

in 1884 included the Tropical, Herbaceous, Greenhouse & Ornamental, Temperate House and Arboretum departments. The work was hard and before mechanized equipment was introduced, tasks were done either by manpower or with the assistance of the Kew horses.

Alongside the gardeners, a variety of scientific staff were employed at Kew. These roles were based in the Herbarium, where the collections of dried plant specimens that document the identity of plants were (and still are) housed, and from 1877 in the Jodrell Laboratory, where plant physiology was studied and, later, plant anatomy and cytogenetics. To support the work of both the horticultural and scientific staff, comprehensive documentary collections were amassed and housed in a library, under the care of the Keeper of the Herbarium. A Curator of the Museums was also employed to manage the various museums, along with administrative staff and attendants. Also listed on 19th- and early 20th-century staff records are roles such as firelighter, medical

officer, porters, gatekeepers, constables, fireman and a 'bell-ringer and water fowl keeper'. These roles reflect the mosaic of different tasks that were required to keep Kew functioning.

For the members of staff, Kew was much more than a place of employment; they were members of the 'Kew family'. Sports and social clubs flourished, the most eminent being the Kew Guild, set up in 1893 to enable former members of staff to keep in touch. Lasting friendships were formed and, with the advent of the employment of women at Kew, some marriages transpired too.

LEFT

J.A. Simon, who worked as a gardener
at Kew during the 1940s, had previously
been a farmer in Alderney, in the Channel
Islands, before fleeing the German
occupation in World War II. Simon's duties
at Kew included cutting hay for the five
Suffolk Punch horses used in the Gardens.

ABOVE

Transplanting large trees to alter and enhance both public and private landscapes was common during the 19th century, but the practice often resulted in damage to the tree, with the consequence that the effect tended to be short-term. William Barron (1805–91), who began his career as a gardener at the Royal Botanic Garden Edinburgh, sought a solution to this problem after taking up a post at Elvaston Castle, landscaping its grounds for the 4th Earl of Harrington. His employer requested that he move a large tree, and Barron, realizing that previous methods would not be adequate, set about devising his Tree Transplanter – a horse-drawn machine that would allow such specimens to be carried distances of up to 32km (20 miles) without causing them harm.

ABOVE

Before it was transported, a tree was prepared several seasons in advance. First a trench was cut around it, severing and confining the expanding roots, and the channel was then filled with a fine soil. Over the next year or so, the roots would enter the excavated area, forming rootlets. When the tree was ready to be removed, this rootball was wrapped in canvas, with wooden planks for support. Here, a prepared tree is moved along using trunks as rollers. Barron's Tree Transplanter improved upon this system, as the machine could be completely dismantled then reconstructed around the tree, which was then winched into place. The process was reversed when it reached its destination. The Transplanter allowed for the transport of trees weighing up to 7 tonnes, which would have been virtually impossible using man-power alone.

RIGHT

Kew's Tree Transplanter was purchased in 1866, and was in use until 1936. The apparatus required about 10 men and three horses to operate it. In 1998, the Kew Friends funded its restoration, and it is the last of its kind in the world.

LEFT

William Dallimore was a well-liked and long-serving
member of staff, with a Kew career spanning more
than 45 years. He joined Kew as a student gardener
in 1891, aged 20, and worked in the Palm House, the
Tropical Propagating Pits and the Arboretum, of which
he became Foreman in 1901. This photograph shows him
as a young man, possibly in his student days, carrying
his tree-pruning equipment. He later became Keeper
of the Museums, established the Wood Museum and
supervised the development of the National Pinetum at
Bedgebury in 1925. He was regarded as one of the leading
authorities on trees and shrubs in the UK. Dallimore also
played a key role in the founding of the Kew Guild. To his
colleagues, he was known as 'good old Dallimore'.

RIGHT

Since its establishment in 1795, the Arboretum has grown
from its original 2 hectares (5 acres) and now covers most
of Kew's 121.5 hectares (300 acres). As the area expanded,
so did the quantity of trees and shrubs; in 1896, the number
of species and varieties was listed at 3000 and by 1924
this had already grown to 6300. Today there are 14,000.
Horticultural methods have changed over the years, partly as
a result of the mechanization of the equipment used. Here,
trees are being moved using a jack and boards on rollers.

It takes trees years to recover from transplantation,
particularly in Kew's sandy, dry soil. This had to be
supplemented with fertilizers, for which manure from the
local omnibus station was used. In the late 1890s, Dallimore
records that farmers could take grass cuttings from the
Gardens for their animals in return for reduced-price manure.

Where trees had developed cavities, dead or decaying
wood was removed before the area was treated with
antiseptic and a coating of coal tar to prevent any parasites.
Any resulting large holes were filled with bricks and a layer
of cement to prevent damp from penetrating (far right).

C.F. Coates, the Arboretum propagator, is shown here taking a bud from a cutting for grafting onto new stock in 1943. This particular cutting was from a descendant of the apple tree in the garden of Woolsthorpe Manor in Lincolnshire, Isaac Newton's birthplace, from which the apple fell that inspired Newton's theory of universal gravitation. As the tree was dying, the National Trust sent cuttings to Kew for propagation. The graft was successful and a young tree was sent back to Woolsthorpe in 1945.

LEFT

This shed was based in the Tropical Department (known as the Tropical Pits), attached to one of the greenhouses. It provided many thousands of plants for the main public glasshouses. Loam, peat and sand, a mixture of which was used for potting young plants, were kept in the bins under the benches. Leaf mould and sheep droppings were also added to the mix, having been collected from the Gardens and nearby parks.

LEFT

Air-layering is a technique that is used to propagate trees and shrubs, particularly those that do not root easily from cuttings. A wound is made on the stem of the plant, which is then wrapped in damp moss and covered with polythene to retain the moisture. This encourages the wrapped area to grow roots, and once they have developed the stem is removed from the main plant and potted up. Here, the technique is being used in the Palm House in 1954. The practice is still used today.

ABOVE

A group of gardeners clean the Orchid House in the old T-Range. Cleaning and maintaining the various glasshouses was a laborious but essential job. While interior staining was produced by humid conditions that caused algae to grow, exterior dirt was exacerbated by local pollution, a particular problem before the Clean Air Act was passed by Parliament in 1956. Remembering his first day at Kew, William Dallimore was shocked to see the extent of the problem: 'The Aroid House . . . looked as though it was covered with slates instead of glass, but it was not until I saw the Ferneries, Greenhouse, Succulent House and T-Range that I fully appreciated the dirt. The glass had not been washed after the fog and it was black with filth. To make things worse the Ferneries were wholly, and some of the other houses partly, glazed with green glass . . . I did not know then what a harmful effect London fog has on plant life that should have been in first-rate condition.'

ABOVE

Washing the windows of 'House No. 10', the Waterlily House, was a more challenging task than in the Orchid House, and required a good sense of balance.

RIGHT

H.W. Sayer, shown here in May 1924, was Sub-Foreman of the Temperate House pits, a complex of nurseries where plants destined for the Temperate House were propagated. The pits were located in the Stable Yard, in an area that was not accessible to visitors, and were replaced in 1993 by a new propagation house which incorporated a boilerhouse.

Throughout the 19th century and well into the 20th, Kew kept one pony and up to seven horses that were used for ploughing, mowing and carrying heavy loads. These working horses occupied two paddocks, one near Lion Gate Lodge, and another in the area where the Banks Building now stands. A resident Horse-Keeper lived in a cottage near the Stable Yard. The favoured variety was the Suffolk Punch, a hardy breed developed in the 1700s for use in agriculture.

ABOVE RIGHT

George Appleby joined Kew as a pony-boy (a stable-hand), at the age of 14 in April 1931, earning 18 shillings a week. After three years he was promoted to the post of Junior Carter, and by 1938 became a full Carter, working for the weekly sum of £2.12.0. He continued to work with the horses until he was transferred to the constabulary in 1951. He retired in 1982.

RIGHT

After a heavy snowfall, the horses were set to work pulling the snow plough. During the winter they were also used to draw carts containing blocks of ice cut from the Lake to replenish stocks in the Ice House, where perishable food was stored. This job was unpopular with the gardeners, and they were bribed with beer.

RIGHT AND ABOVE
Here, George Appleby sits atop the
hay-cart. The hay was derived from
grass collected in the Arboretum.

'They gardened in bloomers the newspapers said,
So to Kew without waiting all Londoners sped;
From the top of the buses they had a fine view,
Of the ladies in bloomers who gardened at Kew.'

From *Fun*, a Victorian weekly satirical magazine

LEFT AND RIGHT

The first female gardeners, Annie Gulvin and Alice Hutchings, were employed at Kew in 1896, having been recruited from Swanley Horticultural College for Women. So as not to distract their male colleagues and to discourage 'sweethearting', the women had to wear a rather unflattering uniform that consisted of brown bloomers, woollen stockings, waistcoats, jackets and peaked caps; two of the female gardeners can just be distinguished from their male colleagues in the group photograph (right). Alice's husband said of her experience at Kew that 'the girls had a hard time in the early days, quite different to that given to women in the two wars', but despite this Alice excelled in her role, becoming a Sub-Forewoman in the Alpine Department. The photograph showing Eleanor Morland, Gertrude Cope and Alice Hutchings (left) dates from 1898. By 1902, all the women gardeners had left to take up horticultural posts elsewhere and it was not until World War I that female gardeners were employed at Kew again.

ABOVE

Annie Gulvin left Kew in 1897 to take up the post of
head gardener on an estate in South Wales. *The Journal
of the Kew Guild* of 1898 reported that she had 'the
distinction of being the first woman to take solo charge
of a garden on exactly the same terms as a man.'

ABOVE

The first four Keepers of the Herbarium, left to right: Professor Daniel Oliver (Keeper 1864–90), W. Botting Hemsley (1899–1908), Dr Otto Stapf (1908–22), and J.G. Baker (1890–99), photographed in 1916. The Keeper is the most senior member of staff in the Herbarium, with responsibility for the Library as well as the Herbarium collections.

ABOVE RIGHT

The senior Gardens staff are seen here in 1902. Left to right: Walter Irving, Foreman, Herbaceous Department; William Watson, Curator of the Gardens; Charles P. Raffill, Foreman, Temperate House; Walter Hackett, Foreman, Tropical Department; William Jackson Bean, Assistant Curator of the Gardens; Arthur Osborn, Foreman Decorative Department; William Dallimore, Foreman, Arboretum.

RIGHT

The Kew Fire Brigade was operated on a voluntary basis by staff from the Gardens, with, from 1882, a station in the Melon Yard on the Kew Road near the southern tip of Kew Green. The entrance, which has long been bricked over, can still be seen along the boundary wall. The service closed down in the 1920s, when the Richmond Fire Brigade assumed responsibility for the Gardens.

ABOVE

The Royal Botanic Gardens Constabulary was established in 1845. Initially, a policeman employed by the Metropolitan force would watch the
Gardens at night, while Kew constables patrolled the Gardens during admission hours. These 'constables' were either part-time gardeners
or Crimean War pensioners, but by 1859 the service officially comprised one policeman, three uniformed constables and two gatekeepers.
Thiselton-Dyer is the white-haired officer carrying a cane in the centre; he often undertook his rounds in full constabulary uniform.

ABOVE AND LEFT

William Thiselton-Dyer was a hugely successful Director of Kew, and also something of an enigma. On his first sighting of the Director, Dallimore describes him as 'a slender man, wearing riding breeches, brown velvet jacket, tweed waistcoat and a Tyrolese hat, who was smoking a cigarette'. Smoking was strictly forbidden in the Gardens, with the exception of the man who made the rules, the Director.

In his memoirs, Dallimore recalls a story regarding Thiselton-Dyer's sense of style. In the 1890s, the student gardeners wore cloth suits to work in. After ruining yet another suit, Dallimore bought himself a cheap pair of corduroy trousers and a blue linen jacket. On seeing him in this ensemble, Thiselton-Dyer pulled Dallimore aside and asked him where the trousers were from. Within a few days, Thiselton-Dyer was to be seen in cords, a trend that was shortly followed by the other more senior staff.

ABOVE

Thiselton-Dyer was knighted in 1899 and here he wears court dress, with his Order of St Michael and St George.

RIGHT

On becoming Director, Thiselton-Dyer appointed himself Inspector of the Kew Constabulary, a title that is still held by serving directors, and acquired a constabulary uniform.

Once a year, Kew employees are gathered together for the staff photograph. These examples, representing images taken approximately every 20 years, provide an insight into the changing fashions and demographics of those at work in the Gardens. In the example taken during World War I, there are greater numbers of women, all of whom are gone by the following photograph. The photograph also illustrates how the working life began much earlier, with young boys present among the staff.

RIGHT

1878

RIGHT

1893

William Macdonald Campbell (seated on the left) was Curator of the Gardens from 1937 to 1960. Every morning he would hold meetings with his assistants to discuss daily matters, including plants received and due for dispatch, as well as distributing specimens sent in by the public for identification. During the 1940s, his team were, from left to right, Arthur Osborn (Deputy Curator and Arboretum), Charles P. Raffill (Temperate House), Lewis Stenning (Tropical House, taking over from Campbell as Curator in 1960), Sydney A. Pearce (Decorative Department), and R. Holder (Herbaceous and Alpine Department).

ABOVE

John Hutchinson was Keeper of Museums from 1936 to 1948, curating Economic Botany collections and advising British ministries and colonial governments. Here he is referring to dried specimens in the Herbarium while working on his revision of George Bentham and Joseph Hooker's great work, *Genera Plantarum*, first published in 1862. In the 19th century, Bentham had estimated there to be 7500 genera of flowering plants, and describing all of them had been a demanding task for even these two most capable scientists. When Hutchinson took up the baton, there were 11,500 known genera, and he approached the task almost single-handed. It was planned as a 10-volume work, but Hutchinson's *Genera of Flowering Plants* was published in three volumes in 1964, 1967 and posthumously in 1972.

ABOVE

Here, two members of staff are at work in the Mounting Room. Once collected specimens have been dried and pressed, they are mounted onto a herbarium sheet of archival quality paper, with an identifying label in the bottom right-hand corner. The label indicates the specimen's origin, the collector, the family and genera numbers, and the plant's botanical name, as well as other information such as local uses. Specimens are then arranged in cupboards according to family, region, genus and species. Ancillary collections are cross-referenced; these include the carpological collection, comprising mainly fruits but also parts too large to fit onto a herbarium sheet, and the spirit collection, which houses fragile items such as orchid flowers that would otherwise lose their formal integrity.

The representation of plants has traditionally been through paintings and drawings, and even today, in the age of photography, botanical illustration remains a vital tool for botanists presenting a new species to their peers. Yet photography cannot convey the entirety of the plant in the same way that an illustration is capable of, for example depicting fruit and flowers on the same specimen, singling out particular features important in its identification, intricately describing minute components to scale and isolating elements in a scientific context. Over the years many artists have lent their creative skills to Kew, from Franz Bauer, 'Botanick Painter to His Majesty' in the reign of King George III, to the talented men and women who contribute to contemporary flora. Here are four exponents of this art form.

LEFT

Walter Hood Fitch, born in 1017 in Lanark, Scotland, was apprenticed to a calico designer when he met William Hooker in 1832, while mounting specimens in his free time. Hooker, who was then professor of Botany at the University of Glasgow and editor of *Curtis's Botanical Magazine*, sent Fitch some illustrations to copy and was so impressed by his talent for drawing, composition, swiftness and precision that he bought out the young artist's apprenticeship. Thus began Fitch's long association with the *Botanical Magazine* and with Kew: over the next 40 years he produced illustrations for more than 2700 plants for the *Magazine*, and published more than 10,000 in total. Fitch was so adept in the art of lithography, where the image for printing is produced by drawing with an oil or wax-based medium on to a metal or stone plate, that he would work directly onto the surface without making preliminary sketches.

RIGHT

Stella Ross-Craig, born in 1906, received an early induction into plant life from her father, a botanist, who taught his young daughter to identify wild flowers. At 18, she enrolled at Thanet Art School, studying life drawing, print-making, photography and embroidery, as well as attending evening classes in botany. In 1929, she began contributing to *Curtis's Botanical Magazine* and went on to submit more than 300 illustrations over the next 50 years. Her virtuosity for working in black and white is most effectively displayed in what is probably her exceptional work, *Drawings of British Plants*. Produced between 1948 and 1973, it incorporates all native species excluding grasses and sedges, comprising 1316 plates in 31 parts.

After Fitch's departure from Kew, Joseph Hooker set about finding a new artist to replace him on the *Botanical Magazine*. Matilda Smith, Hooker's second cousin, was a proficient artist but had no prior knowledge of botany, so she was appointed under his tutelage. She took up the post in 1877 at the age of 23 and remained in Kew's employ for the next 45 years, producing more than 2300 drawings for the *Magazine*. At first, like Kew's other artists, she was paid for each work submitted, but by 1898 she was the *Magazine's* sole artist and was officially entered onto the payroll, becoming the Civil Service's first Botanical Artist. In 1916 she became president of the *Kew Guild*, and in 1921 was accepted as an Associate of the Linnean Society – the second woman to achieve this honour. Smith paid tribute to her cousin by designing the floral reliefs that appeared on his memorial, which resides in St Anne's Church on Kew Green.

RIGHT

Ann Webster studied at Guildford Art School before becoming a freelance botanical artist, contributing to *Curtis's Botanical Magazine*, *Flora of Tropical East Africa*, and other Kew publications. Here she can be seen sketching a live specimen of *Eulophia horsfallii*, a spectacular tall-growing orchid with purple flowers. The photograph, taken in 1951, illustrates the logistical difficulties botanical artists often face when approaching their subject.

LEFT

Charles Metcalf became Keeper of the Jodrell Laboratory in 1930. Initially, the only other member of staff was a laboratory assistant, and together they worked on plant anatomy, as well as providing an identification service for plant specimens. Here, Metcalf is identifying a timber specimen. The Laboratory was occasionally called upon by the police to identify samples of plant materials found at crime scenes. These included sawdust, which was often used to line safes, and clung to the clothes of safebreakers.

RIGHT

As the functions of the Jodrell Laboratory expanded, so did the numbers of staff employed. By 1960, Metcalf had a staff of three; as Cytology and Physiology departments were added, a new building was constructed, and by 1964 there were 20 permanent members of staff. This photograph dates from 1963 and was taken outside the old Jodrell Laboratory. Metcalf can be seen in the centre.

Before 1969, Kew's Library was situated in Hunter
House, the oldest part of the building. It was
open to British and overseas students, and to
visiting researchers. Seated at the table are, on
the left, Samuel O'Tule, a visiting student from
Uganda, and right, Pat Brenan, who was Head of
the African section in 1959 when this photograph
was taken. In 1965, Brenan became Keeper of the
Herbarium and Deputy Director of the Gardens.

ABOVE

Working at Kew has always had a strong social aspect. The Kew Guild was established in 1893 as 'an association of past and present members of staff of the Royal Botanic Gardens, Kew'. Initially, membership was restricted to those who worked in some kind of horticultural role, but eventually all members of staff were allowed to join. Ever since its inception, the Guild has awarded annual prizes to students and published a journal that shares information about what many consider their alma mater. It has also hosted an annual dinner; this image is of the 1905 event, which was held at the Holborn Restaurant. In the 21st century, the Guild still brings together former and current members of staff.

The Kew Botany Club was set up in 1892, providing an opportunity for those who did not work in the Herbarium to study botany. It was also hoped that the Club would encourage gardening staff to collect specimens for the Herbarium. Prizes were offered for the best collections. Here, some of the members of the 1956 Club are seen on the Annual Outing, which was to Dungeness that year, where members collected in the dunes and on the beach. This photograph was taken by F. Nigel Hepper, the Club's President in 1956, and shows Jim O'Shea, Tim Harvey, Allen Paterson and Trevor Elton. Hepper writes in his 1956 review of the Club that the Annual Outing was 'a fascinating and rewarding day' ending 'at Rye, where tea was taken'.

LEFT

During World War II, the Kew Guild's annual dinner was replaced by a tea party as a result of rationing and the absence on military service of so many of the Gardens' staff. The tea party shown here was hosted in the Director's garden in 1946. In *The Journal of the Kew Guild* for this year it is recorded that 'the Annual Tea has proved so popular that this might still be kept as a permanent reminder of happy gatherings spent under war-time conditions. Food problems make the chances of a 1948 Dinner rather remote'.

Running, tennis, netball, swimming, cricket and football clubs were a major part of Kew's flourishing social scene, as well as more sedentary activities such as the pudding club. Details of the Cricket Club were included in the very first edition of *The Journal of the Kew Guild*, in 1893, which stated that 'the Kew Gardeners' Cricket Club probably does more to keep the gardeners in health than the official medical officer'. In 1893, two half-day Saturday matches were played with the Kew Village Club during the season, plus a number of evening matches, including games of 'North v. South' and 'Smokers v. Non-Smokers'.

RIGHT

Cricket Club, 1933

RIGHT

Tennis Club, 1908

Kew at War

During the two World Wars, life at the Gardens went on with remarkably little disruption. In World War I the Gardens' maintenance and daily routine was disturbed, but this was most probably due to the replacement of the established gardeners by volunteer staff and it was not an enduring problem. At the outbreak of World War II, the Gardens closed to the public while the reduced staff were redeployed and air raid shelters for staff and visitors were constructed, but they were soon reopened and attendance actually exceeded peacetime numbers. Irreplaceable library items were evacuated to Oxfordshire and Gloucestershire.

During both wars, lawns were dug up as households were urged to 'Dig for Victory', and public land (including Kew Green) was given over to allotments in the drive to make Britain self-sufficient. The Gardens assumed a new function, creating a 'model' allotment which sought to instruct the public on the best way to produce their own vegetables and making some of the land available to local residents for their use. Research at Kew became more directly concerned with the war effort, the botanists turning their attention to finding alternatives to food crops and medicinal plants that could no longer be imported and experimental work such as the application of nettle fabric for reinforcing plastic in aircraft construction.

More than 30 women gardeners were employed at Kew during World War I, with the majority of them remaining until 1918 and some staying on until 31 March 1922, when the employment of women gardeners was terminated. During the next war, conscription of women into war work became compulsory in Britain in 1941 and women were once again called upon to fill the roles left vacant at Kew, this time in greater numbers than before.

Thirty high-explosive bombs fell onto the Gardens during the Blitz. Whether the site was considered a legitimate target is interesting, given that Chambers' Pagoda had been converted to test the aerodynamics of bombs; the Royal Aircraft Establishment sent its bomb designers to drop small models of shells through holes cut through each of the floors, recording their performance.

In 1941, a bomb fell very close to the Pagoda without causing damage. However, other bombs broke glass in the Temperate House, the Palm House, North Gallery and Museum No. 1. In the course of a night raid on 24–25 September 1940, 121 panes of glass were lost in the Herbarium and Library, which nevertheless remained open to visitors for the duration of the conflict. The Waterlily House also suffered considerable bomb damage, though the only direct hit was on the Stableman's House. Volunteer fire-fighters and staff were on standby every night from 1 September 1939 until 24 March 1945.

On Peace Day in July 1919, two oaks and a horse chestnut, grown from seeds collected from the Verdun battlefields in France in 1917, were placed close to Museum No. 1. One of the oaks was planted close to Chambers' Temple of Arethusa, which became a memorial for the fallen of the two world wars.

ABOVE

The number of visitors to the Gardens increased from 825,372 in 1941 to 1,401,001 in 1943 as people
sought a temporary diversion from the hardships and uncertainties of life on the Home Front; the restriction
on long-distance travel meant that Kew was a popular destination for Londoners seeking a day out.
This photograph, taken in about 1940, shows visitors to one of Kew's demonstration plots.

ABOVE

In December 1915, *The Journal of the Kew Guild* reported that 'The Great War has overshadowed everything during the past nine months'. At the AGM that year, the *Journal* recounted, the Chairman had proposed a toast to His Majesty's Forces, commenting that 'Kewites were trying to do their share' and he was 'pleased to see the now familiar khaki represented in the room'. With the exception of one married labourer, all members of staff who were of military age (under 40) and fit for service had enlisted in the forces. Women took many of the roles; in 1915 alone, of 38 regular gardeners, 24 were women.

ABOVE

William B. Turrill began working as an assistant in the Herbarium in 1909. In 1915, he joined the Sanitary division of the Royal Army Medical Corps, which was responsible for maintaining sanitation of the Corps' barracks, kitchens and living quarters. The position was held only by well-educated, highly skilled personnel, sometimes drawn from the professional classes.

ABOVE

Joseph Reardon joined the staff as a gardener in July 1914, having trained at Tully Nurseries, Kildare. He attended Kew's 'Mutual Improvement Society', scoring the highest number of marks in Economic Botany, and in October 1914 he lectured on 'Alpines in Ireland' for the same course. In October 1915, he left to become an Assistant at Cambridge Botanic Gardens, Massachusetts, where he was appointed Curator four years later. He is portrayed here during his wartime naval service.

LEFT

Nothing is known about this soldier, one of the many Kew staff who signed up to fight in World War I, except that his name was Frank and he had links to Fermoy in County Cork, Ireland. *The Journal of the Kew Guild* printed letters from former employees serving in the forces, providing a platform for them to recount their experiences. One, from W.F. Godfrey on the Western Front, told of how he and his comrades had 'almost a feeling of pity for any of the enemy who are unfortunate enough to be in the trenches. All the time the usual flares light up the scene, but what's that! rockets? . . . we watch them bursting. The showers of green and other coloured stars give one the impression of a Crystal Palace firework display . . . stray bits of shrapnel fly unpleasantly close, a whirring note heralding their approach'. The allusion to home and to the Crystal Palace, Joseph Paxton's other masterpiece, bring a particular poignancy to this entry. Each year the Journal would print a list of servicemen from Kew's staff, past and present, noting those killed in action, including an occasion where two employees lost their lives in France on the same day: 'Sergeant H.J. Smith, a garden labourer, and Private F. Windebank, pony boy, both of the East Surrey Regiment.'

RIGHT

William Nesfield's parterre outside the Palm House took on a new role as food crops replaced floral displays. In the 1915 issue of *The Journal of the Kew Guild*, the following poem appeared under the title 'Our Roll of Honour, Gardeners of Empire'. Signed simply 'H.H.T.', it was probably by Harry H. Thompson, editor of the journal *The Gardener*. He was a former gardener who had left Kew in 1899.

'Tillers of the soil they were – just gardeners then,
In faith the day's work doing as the day's work came,
Peaceful art in peace pursuing – not seeking fame –
When through the Empire rang the Empire's call for men.

Gardeners they were, finding in fragile flowers delight,
Love in frail leaves, and charm even in wayside weeds.
Who, in their wildest dreams, ne'er rose to do brave deeds,
Defending righteous cause against relentless Might!

The wide world gave her flowers for them – the mountains high,
The valleys low, and classic hills all fringed with snow
Where fires by sunset kindled light the alpen-glow.
O! Fate implacable! – to see those hills and die!

The war god rose refreshed – Gardeners and soldiers then!
Who, that slumbering Peace might wake, dared, with manhood's zeal,
To make Life's sacrifice to Love's supreme appeal.
For King and Country fought and died – Gardeners and Men!

RIGHT

This photograph shows Kew's women gardeners in November 1916. By 1918, the conflict had endured for four years and women's roles had continued to grow; they worked in the Herbarium as Assistants alongside men, while in the gardens, three women held posts as foremen. Of a staff of 34 gardeners, 23 were women. Lucy Joshua was one of those who joined Kew in 1915, and at first she found the work 'dull . . . trimming edges and helping to push round a heavy and very lop-sided mower . . . but we felt it was war work and kept cheerful'. She recalled how women worked in every department except for the Palm House, though most were consigned to the Decorative Department. Here, women were so numerous that it earned the name of 'Coutts' harem', its Foreman being John Coutts. The women gardeners would have been experienced, having trained at institutions that included Swanley Horticultural College, Regent's Park Botanic Gardens, and Kew, and although their presence was greeted with suspicion at first by their male colleagues, Lucy remembered that once they had 'shown them that we were prepared to do our full share . . . the ice was broken and there was real comradeship'. However, by 1922, their presence on the Kew staff lists had disappeared, although some of the female Herbarium staff remained.

Back row, left to right: K.W. Harper, I.L. Lines, H.A. Rowan, M.I. Yeo, N.J. Watson, E.M. Harper, K. Watson. Middle row, left to right: H.W. Davidson, N.M. Wiltshire, C. Nash, V.H. Harvey, E.M. Casey, H.M. Ranson, A. Hutchings, C.F. Ellis, M.W. Watson. Front row, left to right: A.B. Freda, N. Robshaw, I.E. Clark, L.H. Joshua, R.M. Williams, E. Stubington, V.S. Bell, M.E. Goad, M.N. Owen, N. Grant.

ABOVE

The German naval campaign led to food shortages and common land was often used to create allotments, as is shown in this photograph of Kew Green, taken in 1917. The church is St Anne's, which has a long association with the Gardens; both William and Joseph Hooker are buried in the churchyard, and memorial tablets to both men reside within its walls.

RIGHT

Sandbag walls were put in place to protect the Herbarium in 1939. Sandbags were generally used as a temporary defence method, and there were guidelines for their use.

LEFT

This photograph, taken in the autumn of 1939, shows the observation post in Cambridge Cottage Garden. Following Britain's declaration of war on Germany in September 1939, there was an absence of any real military action on both sides for some while. The public perception was that nothing of importance was happening, but people were still required to prepare for the possibility of invasion; a strict blackout was put into effect and rationing was introduced on petrol and, later, food. Observation posts, where soldiers were placed to monitor possible enemy movement, were assembled throughout the country. Some of these were temporary buildings such as this one, made from wood and sandbags, while others can still be found around the countryside today.

ABOVE

Elsie Wakefield, a botanist in the Herbarium, and Miss Minnie Hill, a female gardener in the Tropical Propagating Department, are seen here sewing blankets in the entrance to the Herbarium's first-aid post. According to a Ministry of Agriculture missive sent to all ARP personnel, before leaving the first-aid post, serious casualties were to be marked by indelible pencil or lipstick on the forehead with a letter 'T' for tourniquet, 'M' for morphis, 'H' for haemorrhage, 'C' for gas contamination and 'X' for any other condition requiring the immediate attention of a doctor.

RIGHT

The Government-issued Anderson shelter was named after Sir John Anderson, who, as Lord Privy Seal, was responsible for coordinating air raid defences. This shelter, near the Palace nursery, was photographed during construction, illustrating the panels of curved and corrugated galvanized steel that were the basis of the structure. This was covered with about 1.5m (5ft) of soil, giving it the capacity to absorb large amounts of energy and so protecting those within from bomb blasts.

RIGHT

Here, William Turrill is modelling the full gas protection suit usually worn by Air Raid Wardens. In the spring of 1940, a Local Defence Volunteer Company (later Home Guard) was set up in Richmond, with so many of the Gardens' staff joining that a Kew Gardens Platoon was soon formed, numbering 60 members, with Sir Geoffrey Evans, Economic Botanist, as its Commander, and J. Robert Sealy, Assistant Botanist, as Platoon Sergeant. Meanwhile, Turrill oversaw the evacuation of Kew's Herbarium specimens and books to Oxford, and was recruited to the Intelligence Division of the Admiralty on an unspecified 'botanical assignment'.

ABOVE

The Ministry of Agriculture launched its famous 'Dig for Victory' campaign a month after the outbreak of the war. Britons were encouraged to convert their gardens into allotments to supply crops for their own families and neighbourhoods. For those with no garden, land in public parks was made available, transforming whole cityscapes. By 1943, more than one million tonnes of vegetables were grown in these allotments. Kew did its bit, turning sections of the Gardens over to growing produce, and providing training on how to cultivate food crops; here a demonstration is given on the best methods for sowing peas.

RIGHT

The Model Allotment Plan initiated by the Ministry of Agriculture was designed to provide a household of five people with a year-round supply of vegetables, with the exception of potatoes, in a small area. This model allotment, in front of the Orangery to make it easily accessible to visitors, was intended to be imitated by private growers. Despite its exposed location, it yielded an assortment of vegetables including peas, runner beans, carrots, leeks, onions and tomatoes, a variety of herbs, and fruit such as apples and pears.

ABOVE

Sydney Albert Pearce, Assistant Curator of the Decorative Department, gives a talk at the Demonstration Plot in front of Kew Palace, 1940. At the outbreak of war, Pearce assumed supervision of the Gardens' food plots and allotments. Many of the lawns were ploughed for crop use, and tomatoes were grown in parts of the glasshouses.

LEFT

The potato's capacity to yield greater quantities per acre than comparable crops made them extremely important to the war effort. However, supplies of seed potatoes were insufficient to meet demand, so the Ministry of Food approached Kew to provide a solution. William Campbell, Curator of the Gardens, carried out a number of experiments to assess the potential of cultivating potatoes using slices from the tuber instead. It was found that this method was not only successful, but produced better results. Here, Campbell inspects a newly harvested batch.

RIGHT

To make them light enough to be transported by plane, the tuber slices were dried out in trays of peat for two weeks before being sent to Malta, Cyprus and Palestine. There they could be planted to replace supplies cut off by war, thus freeing up potato crops in Britain. The importance of this work was stressed during a press conference held by Sir Geoffrey Evans, Economic Botanist at Kew, at the Ministry of Agriculture in November 1943; he emphasized the scheme was 'specifically applicable to demand from the Colonies', where potato production was 'greatly hampered by difficulties and delays of sending normal seed potatoes by ship in wartime'.

RIGHT

Here, botanist Mary Ruth Fussel Jackson Taylor is working in the Herbarium in 1939. Women had been among the Herbarium staff in scientific, artistic and clerical roles even before the war. Although their numbers experienced a dip during the post-war years, they continued to have a steadily increasing presence and made a valuable contribution.

RIGHT

Here, botanist Mary Ruth Fussel Jackson Taylor is working in the Herbarium in 1939. Women had been among the Herbarium staff in scientific, artistic and clerical roles even before the war. Although their numbers experienced a dip during the post-war years, they continued to have a steadily increasing presence and made a valuable contribution.

LEFT

Women played an essential role in the country's success in the War, filling gaps left by men called up to the military. At Kew, women were recruited to replace male gardeners, although, as in many areas of working life, their numbers reduced rapidly in 1946 to accommodate men returning from action.

In 1939 *The Journal of the Kew Guild* reported that 'women gardeners have come to Kew once more after an interval of nearly a quarter of a century, and though the costume has changed considerably, the fashion in clogs remains the same, as certain well-preserved specimens can testify. These clogs may now be seen and heard in most departments of the Gardens.' Fourteen women enrolled onto the staff in 1940, and were joined in 1941 by a further thirteen. Most had previously trained as gardeners, while others arrived at Kew via the Auxiliary Territorial Service and the Women's Land Army.

LEFT

Some of Kew's female staff are shown here in 1942. Back row, left to right: Jessie F. Pedgrift, Violet M. Clark, Jean E. Sharps, Frances A. Sharps, Freda Mundy. Middle row, left to right: Olive Horder, Minnie May Hill, Kathleen D. Cornford, Diana A. Hutchinson, Netta Shallcross, Else M. Jensen, Jean M. Thompson, Eileen Fergusson Kelly. Front row, left to right: Constance O. Bell, Myrtle V. Speake, Brenda C. Watts, Eileen Plummer, Betty Cooper, Barbara M. Tarver, E. Victoria Paine, Mary A. Canning, Eunice B. King

ABOVE

The days were long, starting at 6.30am during the summer months, and for new recruits the work could be varied, as shrubberies needed to be tidied, edges clipped and vegetable plots dug. Freda Munday, who began working in the Gardens in July 1941, remarked, 'It's tantalizing to see visitors sitting on a seat enjoying tea at 3pm . . . After ten o' clock when the Gardens open we are a regular Information Bureau and have to face a barrage of questions about vegetable growing. We can help people sometimes and we've become expert too at our self-imposed task of making the public "vegetable-conscious".'

LEFT

In the potting sheds, the day would often start with one of the more junior staff being nominated to scrub the terracotta plant pots which would have been stacked high in a concrete tank the previous day. Other important but menial tasks included crushing and sieving broken crocks for layering at the bottom of the pots to assist drainage. Once the pots were planted up, the gardeners could check whether the plant was adequately watered by tapping the side of the pot. This led to questions from curious visitors, as one gardener, Brenda Watts, reported: 'The other day a visitor asked us why we tapped the pots. "Why," we answered, "if they sound hollow they need a drink." Whereupon the visitor tapped his friend on the shoulder and said: "Ah! Come with me – you need a Worthington!"'

RIGHT

Work in the potting sheds was largely unseen by visitors to the Gardens, but the staff here played a crucial role at Kew as they supplied an array of plants for the great glasshouses and public displays. Hothouse No. 4 exhibited a succession of seasonal flowers, which all had to be prepared in one of the potting sheds. It was exacting work, as one gardener, Victoria Paine, related: 'We help to supply No. 4, and you have no idea what an amount of stuff is required. Although there are many old-established plants in the centre of the house the stages have to be filled with pot plants all the year round . . . A more or less definite plan has to be worked out in advance each year. It would be tragic to run short of flowers or to have gaps!'

RIGHT

The women gardeners arriving at Kew quickly integrated into the workforce, encouraged by the generosity and support of male colleagues who were not used to working alongside women. One gave her first impressions of her new job, saying, 'I came in December, and after I had been officially and very charmingly welcomed by the Director I felt quite at home. I realized we should be very much in the public eye, and very soon the public turned up in force, especially during the weekends . . . The public ask all kinds of questions about the growing of flowers and vegetables, and bring bits of plants to be identified. We find people genuinely interested in Kew, and also as to how we women are getting on. They criticize our colour schemes and the arrangements of the plants . . . But, on the other hand, we are often congratulated.'

In 1939, *The Journal of the Kew Guild* reported on its new members, declaring 'It is seven months since the first arrivals started their duties . . . all trained women. . . taking the place of men and students who have been called up for service in the armed forces. They are employed in the Propagating Pits, Decorative Department, Flower and Rock Gardens, and in certain sections of the Tropical Department, where they can each apply their own particular experience.' Acknowledging that the new women gardeners were as skilled as the men they replaced, the writer refers to the conventional chauvinism of the time, adding, 'by endeavouring to set up a high standard of work, [they will] disprove the saying for all time that the *Nepeta mussinii* is the only plant a woman can't kill! In fact, the Kew women gardeners are now part of the Kew landscape.'

Before arriving at Kew, Brenda Watts trained at Swanley Horticultural College and spent six years working at an experimental farm in Ottowa, Canada. Here, she harvests rose hips, which, prepared as a syrup, became a valuable source of vitamin C during the War, thanks to research carried out at the Gardens.

'Now Adam was a gardener, and God who made him sees
That half a gardener's proper work is done upon his knees;
But with Adam gone to fight the foe and only home on leave
The proper one to kneel and plant and grow our food is – EVE!'

Kathleen 'Kit' Cornford, Kew gardener, 1941–43

ABOVE

Wartime circumstances increased the amount of work carried out at Kew, including research into increasing crop ratios and the provision of educational demonstration plots, but the Gardens still needed to be maintained. Government policy emphasized the need for public parks and gardens to sustain their displays of interesting plants for recreational requirements, representing a place for escapism where visitors could see rare, exotic and beautiful plants such as orchids and bromeliads. However, with such an abrupt and complete change of staff, there were some concerns in the 'departments under glass' that despite their competence and enthusiasm the women gardeners lacked the experience to adequately care for such varied and extensive collections, of which orchids were felt to be the most vulnerable.

ABOVE

While opportunities for women at the Gardens were enhanced by the war, it was still difficult for them to rise through the ranks. By 1944, although women dominated the Gardens staff, they were not readily promoted, with only one Assistant Forewoman, Victoria Paine, in the Decorative Department. The following year, she became Acting Assistant Curator of the same Department, the most senior position a woman gardener had ever risen to, but this trend did not last. At the end of the War, the number of women gardeners declined and none were listed in 1952. Even Paine left in 1948 to take up a post teaching horticulture in Putney. Women did return to the Gardens' staff in 1954, but it would be many years before their numbers matched those in wartime.

LEFT

Writing in *The Journal of the Kew Guild* in 1941, Betty Cooper, a gardener who had previously been employed at a plant nursery in Geneva, interviewed a number of the other female gardeners and shared their experiences. She discovered that 'though a few of the younger ones might be a trifle over-awed, all seem to have fallen naturally into the jobs allotted to them' and were 'successful in aspects of gardening varying from stone-breaking for the rock garden to the fine technique of orchid pollination – one more proof of the adaptability of the female'.

RIGHT

The women referred to their uniform of apron
and clogs as their 'battledress'. The clogs were
wooden-soled shoes with leather uppers, and
were considered to afford better protection on
wet glasshouse floors than rubber soles. One of
the gardeners, Jean Thompson, told colleague
Betty Cooper, 'My most vivid impression was the
difficulty I had balancing on the rocks in my clogs.'

RIGHT

Here the women take a moment
to relax from their work, but a
tea-break was instigated only after
Minnie Hill made a personal appeal
to the Director, Sir Arthur Hill, and
just 10 minutes each afternoon
was allowed. Left to right: Else
Jensen, Margaret Lancaster,
Betty Cooper, unidentified,
Jean Sharps, Frances Sharps.

When the War ended it was assumed that women would return to the home to take up the roles that had previously been expected of them. Some, particularly those employed to perform menial or repetitive tasks, were keen to return to the normality of life that war had denied them, but many were sorry to leave their jobs as they enjoyed the stimulation, camaraderie and independence that employment provided. Although many of the women gardeners left Kew, some went on to work in other horticultural positions: Helen Stont, for example, joined the Royal Botanic Garden in Edinburgh, Ruth Mabrose took up a position with the Imperial Bureau of Plant Breeding and Genetics in connection with the Empire Potato Collection, and others found employment in private gardens.

LEFT

For many women, their wartime post at Kew was their first experience of paid work; it was also the first time many visitors to the Gardens would have seen women working in such a public space. One gardener, Jean Thompson, who worked in the Rock Garden, said that she would hear cries of, 'Look at the lady gardeners! – Employing women now, I see – Do you like your work?' to which the visitors volunteered their own answer, without waiting for the women's response, 'We do.'

ABOVE LEFT

A.K. Jackson joined the Herbarium staff as a Technical Assistant in 1930, and served in the Royal Air Force from 1939 to 1945.

ABOVE RIGHT

John Wilfred Sutch, born 8 November 1923, worked as a gardener in the T-Range, Palm House and Arboretum. At the age of 18, he left Kew to join the army, joining the 1st Northants Yeomanry as a tank driver. He served in Normandy in the summer of 1944, and was killed during the battle for Falaise Gap. *The Journal of the Kew Guild* described him as 'knowledgeable, conscientious,' and as displaying 'considerable promise'.

ABOVE

Although air raids over Kew were not as relentless as those suffered by the East End of London, the area was still afflicted by the War. The Gardens escaped with only inconsequential damage to the buildings, but the surrounding streets suffered more severely, as seen in this image of Kew Road, just outside the Gardens, In total, 19 civilians in the local community lost their lives during the Blitz, and many more lost their homes and possessions.

LEFT

In 1917, *The Journal of the Kew Guild* reported that 150 of its members were serving in the forces, and 35 had lost their lives by the end of the war. Their names, ranks and regiments were recorded on a commemorative tablet in bronze installed in the Temple of Arethusa, which was accorded the status of Kew's War Memorial. The site was chosen as its position, between Victoria Gate and Museum No. 1, was in an accessible part of the Gardens, and the structure itself supplied a shelter and resting place for relatives of the fallen. An additional plaque to commemorate those who were killed in action during World War II was unveiled on Armistice Day 1951, adding 14 further names to the memorial.

Kew in the Post-war Years

During the post-war era, Kew underwent some dynamic changes. Despite facing a period of austerity, the organization added new buildings, transformed and conserved others, and led major projects of world-wide significance. In the immediate post-War period, under the directorship of Sir Edward Salisbury (1943–56), plants were replaced – including some of Kew's historic trees – and collections were returned from the off-site stores, at a time of great financial constrictions. Taking over the directorship after the sudden death of Sir Arthur Hill in 1943, Salisbury's first act in the post had been to produce a lime-rich habitat near the ice house, augmenting Kew's English Flora collections. His own interest in British plants led him to visit bomb sites to record the flowers he found there.

Salisbury made a journey to the Antipodes in 1949, following which the Australian government offered the generous gift of a new glasshouse to the Gardens. This prefabricated structure, erected in 1952, was to provide much-needed accommodation for Kew's antipodean collections. However, while such new additions to the Gardens were welcome, it was essential that the buildings damaged during the war were restored and although Kew had got off relatively lightly, some buildings required particular attention. The Waterlily House, which had sustained the worst damage, was not fully restored until 1965, as there were more pressing matters. The Palm House had been poorly maintained for some years; finally it was judged unsafe, and closed to the public in 1952. Initially developers argued in favour of demolition and replacement, with a number of schemes being mooted, but thankfully restoration and renewal were finally approved and the building reopened in 1957, two years before the Gardens' bicentennial celebrations.

Post-war, Kew renewed its close ties with other gardens and botanical stations all over the world, collecting, dispatching and propagating species with economic value, but this time working collaboratively rather than as an imperial master. Geoffrey Evans, Kew's Economic Botanist, took part in a scheme to introduce high-yielding food plants from Peru to East Africa, and in 1951 a new quarantine house was constructed using financial support from a colonial development and welfare grant. Scientists at Kew also embarked upon the *Flora of Tropical East Africa*, a project that would turn out to be a massive undertaking.

Kew continued to collect and document the world's species and was quickly outgrowing its facilities. When Salisbury retired in 1956, Sir George Taylor, former Keeper of Botany at the British Museum, succeeded him, and it was under his administration that Kew acquired a new arboretum in the grounds of Wakehurst Place in the Sussex Weald. Scientific laboratories were expanded and classrooms for horticultural education were created in the new Jodrell building opened in 1965, while the Herbarium acquired a new wing to house its ever-increasing collections. This new wing, opened in 1969, also consolidated the Library,

Art and Archives collections in a single area for the first time in Kew's long history.

John Heslop-Harrison, Director 1971–6, examined the organization's prospective roles and, promoting a cross-disciplinary approach, recommended the establishment of a repository for the world's seeds. This would eventually develop into the Millennium Seed Bank, and in 1971 Roger Smith was appointed Head of Seed Conservation. Through projects such as these, Kew has maintained and augmented its position, leading the way in plant science and horticulture. Its two botanic gardens continue to provide a haven for plants from across the globe, and it is in this context, as a platform for diversity, that the Gardens have the ability to transform and cultivate people's understanding of the natural world.

RIGHT

During the 1950s and '60s, much of the work carried out at Kew centred on the dissemination of plant information and material to botanic gardens and stations across the world. Plants with economic value were of particular consequence. This photograph, taken in 1951, shows banana plants in the foreground and cocoa to the rear, being propagated in the Quarantine House. This was necessary to ensure that they were disease-free before leaving Kew.

LEFT AND BELOW LEFT

When it was constructed, Australia House was larger than all the other glasshouses except for the Temperate House and Palm House. It was a prefabricated building, with a frame of aluminium alloy that would not need replacing or repainting for many years, and was most probably the first of its kind in the world. The building had a roof pitched at an angle to make the most of any winter sunshine for the sun-loving inhabitants. Plants from the dry climate of south-west Australia were moved in from the Temperate House, and Australia House opened to the public in 1952. The house still exists today, although in a different guise; in 1995, the building was remodelled and opened as the Evolution House.

RIGHT

After World War II, Kew began to develop a more collaborative way of working with gardens and scientific organizations around the world. Horticulturalists from overseas came to train at Kew, rather than the colonial botanic gardens relying on the provision of former members of the Kew staff. Here, J.A. Obi from the Nigerian Department of Agriculture is working in one of the Gardens' glasshouses, cutting the flowering spike on an anthurium to stimulate foliage growth.

ABOVE

Shown here are attendees at the Association for the Taxonomic Study of the Flora of Tropical Africa (AETFAT) Conference, Oxford, in 1953. AETFAT was founded in 1951 as a forum for botanists from all nations working on African flora to meet and publish their research. Conferences are held every three years, meeting in a different country each time. The first meeting to be held in Africa was in 1982. This image is from the collection of F. Nigel Hepper, who attended the 1953 Conference as a young botanist from Kew's Herbarium.

LEFT

The Flora of Tropical East Africa (FTEA) was started in 1948 as a project to produce a Flora (guide) to all the plant species growing wild in East Africa. The first volume was published in 1952 and it was not until 2012 that the final, 263rd volume was completed. East Africa has a particularly rich biodiversity and 12,104 plant species from an area of 1,766,000 km² (682sq miles), comprising 3–4 per cent of the world's flora, have been included in the Flora. In order to complete the publication, much field work has been conducted over the decades to collect specimens, many of which were new to science. Although the Flora is published by Kew, it is an internationally collaborative project, with 135 authors from 21 countries. Here botanists are sorting specimens received from East Africa in the Herbarium in 1958.

RIGHT

By the early 1950s, the Herbarium was rapidly running out of space. A report by the Ashby Visiting Group identified the problem and highlighted concerns about duplication of collections at Kew and the Natural History Museum. The two institutions accepted that each should concentrate on particular geographical areas and plant families, and that specific collecting policies should be formulated. As a result of this, in 1959 the Treasury set up a committee chaired by Wilfred Morton to examine the division of collections. An agreement was reached, and the subsequent 'Morton Report' recommended that Kew have responsibility for southern, central and eastern Africa, Madagascar, South America, Australasia, India and South East Asia, while the Natural History Museum would manage collections from the Polar regions, Europe, North West Africa, North and Central America, and the West Indies. In addition, gymnosperms (seed-producing plants) and fungi would be transferred to Kew, while the Natural History Museum would curate bryophytes (non-vascular plants), algae and lichens. Here, Elsie Wakefield, Deputy Keeper of the Herbarium (right), and Arthur Cotton, Keeper of the Herbarium (left), examine fungi brought into the Herbarium for identification.

LEFT

The 20th century brought with it increased mechanization and Kew purchased its first motorized tractor in 1928 to replace a horse that had died. In 1950, the last two chestnut mares to work in the Gardens were purchased, but by 1961 even they had gone and the time of the horse at Kew was at last over.

RIGHT

Harry Ruck, known simply as 'Ruck' to his colleagues, was Kew's packer, and later storekeeper, from 1912 to his retirement in 1959. Here he is seen packing a Wardian case in the early 1950s. For 100 years the Wardian case had been vital in conveying plants around the world, contributing in no small way to botany's advancement as a science. However, it was an increasingly expensive means of transportation, and by the 20th century was restricted to those plants which could not be dispatched by other methods. It finally fell out of use in the 1960s as air freight became a cheaper and swifter option.

LEFT

In the first hundred years after its construction the Palm House gradually fell into disrepair; the warm, humid conditions of the glasshouse had a detrimental effect on the structure, corroding the iron-work and causing it to expand and contract. Consequently, large panes of glass would fall to the floor and improvised temporary solutions were sometimes implemented, as illustrated here. Major refurbishment was carried out in 1929 but it was not enough, and in 1951, an engineer's report recommended that the Palm House should be demolished and rebuilt, in accordance with the post-war ethos of sweeping away the old in favour of the new. In November 1952, the decision was made to close the Palm House to the public.

RIGHT

A number of ideas were submitted for the Palm House, including one proposing that the whole building should be encased within a protective shell. This design by E. Bedford at the Ministry of Works suggested reusing the arches lining the Mall during the Coronation of Queen Elizabeth II in 1953, an idea that was met with hostility in architectural journals. Ultimately, the decision was made to conserve the Palm House and the Gardens retained what is still regarded as its most recognizable, distinctive and symbolic building.

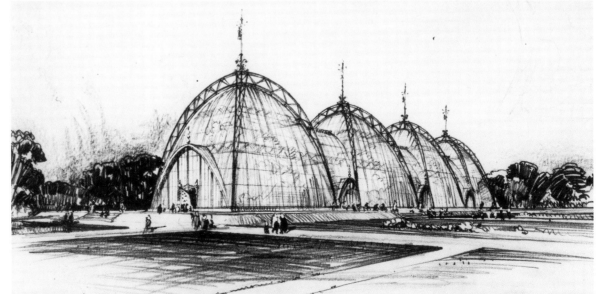

FAR LEFT

Scaffolding encased the great dome as building work progressed. Some of the arches had suffered greatly from corrosion, and in a few cases severe decay was discovered near the feet of the main ribs, a problem that had to be addressed as a matter of urgency. During the restoration, the boilers were converted from coal to oil and relocated to an area adjacent to the Campanile, and the tunnel was modernized to convey hot water to the new heating system.

LEFT

The Palm House remained closed for three years before work commenced, during which time glazing trials were completed. The surviving glass varied in size, and was thought to include some of the original green-tinted panes. All glass was removed and the iron supports were stripped back and repaired. The research recommended that all of the glass be replaced by a custom-made, curved glass that corresponded with the original dimensions; it had been demonstrated that this format raised light levels by a quarter.

RIGHT

In this view of the Palm House during the restoration, the glass has been removed from the central area, laying bare the great iron skeleton. The restoration was carried out one wing at a time, with plant collections repositioned to accommodate the ongoing work.

Once the original paint had been removed an anti-corrosive undercoat was applied to the ribs of the Palm House, over which an ivory-coloured lead-based paint was added.

The Foreman of the Palm House, George Anderson, supervised the preservation of plants. It was an enormous undertaking, requiring a considerable amount of expertise. The collection comprised 1050 species belonging to 63 genera, and was unique in its size and importance. The plants remained in the building throughout the restoration, taking up temporary residence in another part of the Palm House, away from where work was being carried out. When the time came to clear the central transept, only the largest palms remained, 'tubbed-up' and tilted to allow repairs to continue above. The largest tub, measuring 1.8m (6ft) square, was made for the *Brownea* x *crawfordii*, a hybrid that had been in the collection since 1888. In 1957, the transformation of the building was finally completed and work began on restoring the plants to their former homes.

ABOVE

The restored Palm House was reopened by the Queen on 2 June 1959. The total
work, excluding the scaffolding, came to just less than £100,000. At the time
this would have seemed a vast amount of money, but the cost of demolition and
construction of a new building would have come to almost three times that sum,
and Kew would have been deprived of one of its great iconic buildings.

LEFT

In 1959 Kew celebrated its bicentenary, and as part of the celebrations the Queen and Prince Philip visited on 2 June that year. They toured the Gardens, where the paths were lined with staff and invited groups, planted two commemorative trees on the lawn in front of Kew Palace and took afternoon tea in the Orangery. After tea, staff were presented to the royal visitors, who, *The Journal of the Kew Guild* reports, 'took a very keen interest in the work and the responsibilities undertaken by the staff and the establishment generally'. Sally Elizabeth Brown, the eight-year-old daughter of one of the Assistant Curators, presented the Queen with a bouquet of exotic blooms grown at Kew.

RIGHT

During the royal visit, Prince Philip commented on the unkempt appearance of the area between the rear of Kew Palace and the Gardens' boundary wall, which had lain semi-derelict for many years. Following this, it was decided that a garden contemporary to the Palace would be designed, incorporating a parterre enclosed by box hedges, a fountain set in an ornamental pond, a mound, and planting in 17th-century style with a domestic feel. The arcades and steps leading down from the Palace were reinstated, using an 18th-century watercolour by Paul Sandley for reference. The Queen opened the garden in 1969 and it became known as the Queen's Garden.

FAR RIGHT

In 1956, Portland stone replicas of a series of ten heraldic figures known as the Queen's Beasts were placed outside the Palm House. They were copies of plaster statues by sculptor James Woodford that had stood outside Westminster Abbey on the coronation of Queen Elizabeth II, each one displaying the armorial bearings of the new Queen's predecessors.

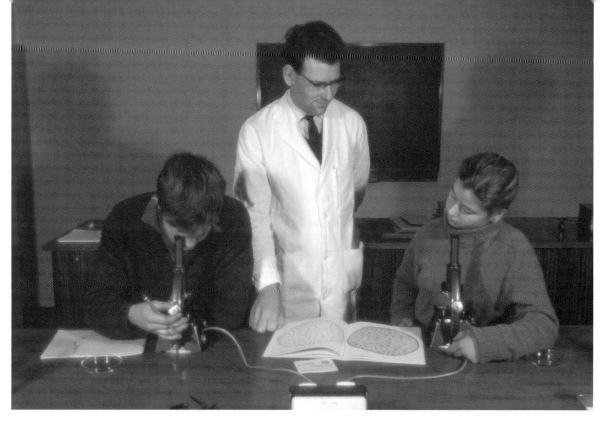

LEFT AND BELOW LEFT

Horticultural training has been a function of Kew for several centuries. During the 19th century, apprentices aged 20–25 with a certain amount of practical experience would come to Kew for two years, working in the Gardens during the day and attending lectures in the evening, held in the Iron Room in the Melon Yard, a cold, uncomfortable building. At the end of their apprenticeship, they would be issued with a written testimonial, later replaced by the Kew Certificate.

In 1963 a three-year Kew Diploma was launched, overseen by a Supervisor of Studies, Leo Pemberton. This course formalized the Gardens' horticultural education, providing an internationally recognized qualification for 20 students a year. Lectures were held in the daytime, in the purpose-built Jodrell Lecture Theatre, which opened in 1965, and a variety of topics were taught in the classrooms shown here. Subjects studied included botany, cell biology, ecology, landscape design, surveying, management, arboriculture, and amenity horticulture, and examinations were held at the end of each year. Practical experience and project work also formed key components of the course and during the first year, students had to keep a vegetable plot.

RIGHT

The Jodrell Laboratory was named after Thomas Jodrell Phillips-Jodrell, the 19th-century philanthropist who financed the original Jodrell building that stood on the site for the preceding 90 years. The Lecture Theatre, shown here, was used for conferences and other staff purposes as well as for students.

TOP LEFT AND ABOVE

The students had their own vegetable plots and were responsible for
constructing scarecrows, often raiding charity shops for suitable clothing.

This series of photographs is from the album of an unknown student. The images depict a number of the social events that formed part of the students' annual calendar.

LEFT

The Clog and Apron Race in 1963; first-year students are dressed for a race down the Broad Walk in the Gardens, wearing the traditional clothes of a gardener – clogs and aprons. The race still takes place today and spectators comment on the thunderous noise that the clogs make as the students hurtle down the path.

LEFT

J. Elsley is shown winning the Kew-Wisley Relay Race, 1965. This is a road race of about 32km (20 miles) from Kew to Wisley, with competing teams from horticultural training establishments. It was first held in 1951 and is still contested today. The race in 1965 was held on 6 March, despite a snowfall of 7.5–10cm (3–4in) a few days beforehand. The Kew team set a new record, completing the course in 92 minutes 51 seconds.

As well as competing in athletics and other sports events, students from Kew and Wisley took part in an annual debate held by the Kew Mutual Improvement Society. This society, established in 1871 to provide horticultural lectures for the apprentice gardeners, still exists today and the lectures are now open to all. Shown here are scenes from before and after the Kew-Wisley Debate of 1965.

BELOW

The 1965 Christmas cabaret and dance was held at the Arosa Rooms, Richmond Ice Rink. Attendance was good and the evening was much enjoyed. A competition was held for the best cabaret act, with the first prize being a bottle of sherry, which went to the Students' Union for their portrayal of five singing beauty queens. *The Journal of the Kew Guild* notes that 'also to be remembered were the Alpine and Herbaceous Department – the singing, guitar-strumming "alpine band"'.

LEFT

Many of the Kew Diploma students have gone on to have illustrious careers, some of them in the media. One of the Diploma's better-known graduates is Alan Titchmarsh, who was on the course from 1969 to 1972. Here he is receiving the Metcalf Cup in 1971. The cup was donated by Charles Metcalf and presented to the students with the best academic results in their second year.

RIGHT

By the 1960s it had become clear that the Jodrell Laboratory was no longer adequate for the type of science that was being studied, nor for the growing number of staff. In 1963 the old building was demolished and replaced with a two-storey laboratory, equipped for studying plant physiology, anatomy, cytology and biochemistry and also containing a lecture theatre. The new building was officially opened in 1965 and state-of-the-art equipment was installed. Metcalf, the Keeper of the Jodrell, wrote of the new building, 'our greatly improved facilities have made possible a great widening and expansion of our activities, and we now have specialists . . . working side by side and helping each other when the necessity arises'.

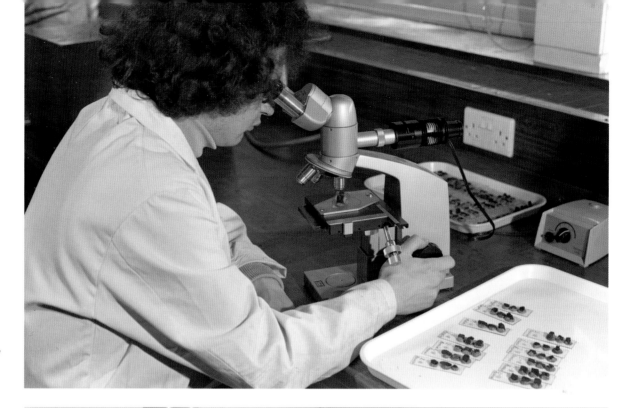

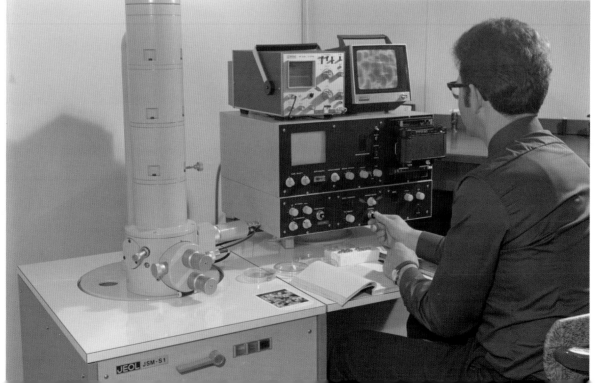

LEFT AND RIGHT

As the collections at Kew developed, it became clear that further space was required and so in 1965 Kew took on the lease of Wakehurst Place in West Sussex, gaining an additional 188 hectares (465 acres). Wakehurst's owner, Sir Henry Price, had previously bequeathed the estate to the National Trust on his death in 1963. Both Price and his predecessor, Gerald Loder, were keen horticulturalists and had developed the estate's garden, creating mostly natural landscaping with temperate woodlands, into which they introduced specimens from the plant-hunting expeditions they had sponsored. The cooler, damp climate and wider range of soil conditions allowed Kew to diversify its plant collections while enhancing the work of the estate's previous owners. The mansion pictured here is the main house on the estate, built in 1590 by Sir Edward Culpeper, a distant relative of Nicholas, the famous herbalist.

RIGHT

The Orangery served as Kew's Wood Museum from 1863, but in May 1957 the new Director, George Taylor, decided to close the building, taking the opportunity to have both its form and original function restored. Over a period of two years, the galleries and staircases were dismantled, the collections of timber removed and redistributed, and the interior restored. Citruses in tubs and plants too large to be housed elsewhere, such as the agave seen here, were introduced, and in 1959 the Orangery reopened.

LEFT

The agave appears to have flourished in the orangery, reaching a height of almost 8m (26ft), and its spike had to be amputated to avoid causing damage to the ceiling. However, as *The Journal of the Kew Guild* reported, the oranges did not thrive, and the building was gravely affected by dry rot. It was not suited to its purpose and within 10 years was badly in need of further conservation, so the plants, including the agave, were removed. Such a fine historic building could not lie empty for long, and it was mooted that it might be put to use as an art gallery, an exhibition space, or even a restaurant. In May 1972, the extensively renovated Orangery reopened as a visitor centre, incorporating an orientation area illustrating the work of the different Gardens' departments, a temporary exhibition space, a bookshop and a picture gallery. The building was restored once again during the 1990s, and its use was again altered, when it reopened as a restaurant in 2002.

LEFT

Two botanists, Jill Cowley and Simon Mayo, both specialists in monocots, use an illustrated book and dried collections to identify a specimen of *Livistona australis* in Wing C of the Herbarium in 1971; monocots are one of the two main groups of flowering plants, and include orchids and palms. Specimens often make their way into the collection through a system of exchange or donation from British and international sources. In turn Kew makes its collections available to visiting scientists and overseas institutions, lending, and in special cases donating, from its own resources. Every specimen must be named, and as curators, botanists study specimens to determine precisely how they may be incorporated into the wider collection. Sometimes a completely new species is discovered, presenting important research material for associated disciplines.

ABOVE

Dried plant material presents a good meal to many animals, especially insects, so it is important that pests in the Herbarium be kept to a minimum. Before the late 1980s a number of pesticides were employed through different applications. This photograph depicts fumigation in the 1970s, probably using methyl-bromide, an organobromine compound that produces a colourless, odourless gas. Unfortunately the gas can be toxic, and if mismanaged it has the potential to cause respiratory and neurological disorders. Today, all specimens entering the collections are frozen for at least 72 hours at -30°C to control infestation.

ABOVE

In the 1960s, Kew's Herbarium collections continued to expand; it was estimated that there were 4.5 million specimens being added at a rate of 50,000–60,000 per year. The building had been extended, on average, every 30 years; the first extension, now referred to as Wing C, was completed in 1877, with Wings B and A following in 1902 and 1932 respectively. But the Herbarium had once again almost reached capacity, and a new building was required. In 1969, Wing D opened, offering a new home for the Fungi and Fern Herbaria, and the carpological and spirit collections. It also provided, for the first time in its history, a dedicated and purpose-built repository for Kew's Library, Art and Archives, which at the time comprised 100,000 books, 250,000 manuscripts and letters, and 160,000 botanical illustrations. The man who oversaw these rich and diverse collections was Ray Desmond, who was Chief Librarian and Archivist at the time, pictured here in his library soon after it opened.

ABOVE

Her Majesty the Queen visits the Herbarium on 14 May 1969, accompanied by Sir George Taylor, Director (centre), and Pat Brenan, Deputy Director and Keeper of the Herbarium and Library, for the official opening of the Wing D extension.

ABOVE

As early as Thiselton-Dyer's directorship (1885–1905), research into storing seeds at low temperatures was taking place.
In the 1960s seed physiology was studied at the Jodrell Laboratory and a seed bank to preserve seeds in refrigerated
conditions was established to facilitate the exchange between Kew and other scientific organizations. In 1974 the physiology
section and seed bank were transferred to Wakehurst Place, where the cold store was housed in the former chapel
of the Mansion (above left). This was the beginnings of what was to become the Millennium Seed Bank Partnership,
the largest ex-situ plant conservation project in the world, which seeks to collect and save seeds of the world's plant
species. The cold store is now housed in a purpose-built structure which consists of laboratories, seed preparation
areas, a public exhibition space, and large underground vaults where seeds are stored at temperatures of -20°C.

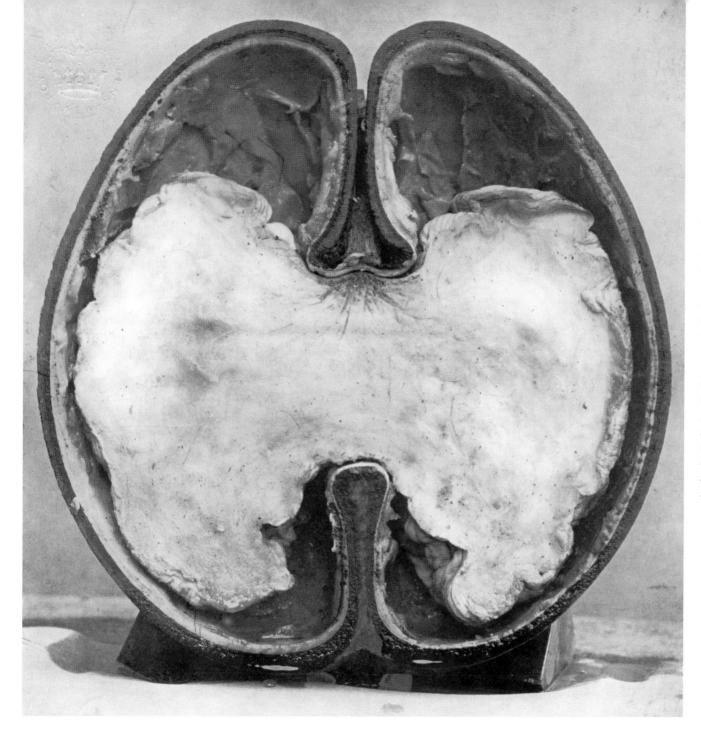

LEFT

The seeds of the coco de mer (*Lodoicea maldivica*), also known as the double coconut, are the largest in the world. They can weigh up to 30kg (66lb) and the plants grow to a huge 30m (98ft), taking 25–50 years to reach maturity. They were discovered growing in the Seychelles in the 18th century and were ascribed magical properties. General Charles Gordon even presented a case to Joseph Hooker that the seeds were the forbidden fruit from the Garden of Eden, partly based on the seed's suggestive shape. The first record of the coco de mer coming to Kew is in 1852, when Mauritius Botanic Garden presented a plant for the Palm House. However, the seeds were notoriously difficult to germinate and the palm is exceptionally tender once grown.

ABOVE AND RIGHT

Because of the commercial value of the seeds, largely based on their attractive, unusual shape and also their use in traditional medicines, the coco de mer has been over-exploited and natural regeneration has virtually ceased. Botanic gardens around the world have striven to propagate the plant and in the 1960s and 1970s the seed was germinated at Kew, after several attempts. Sadly those plants that germinated did not survive for long, not growing much beyond their first few leaves. The plant germinated in the 1970s (above) died after it was moved. It was not until the 1990s that the plant was successfully grown from seed at Kew, aided by warming the rooting zone to 25°C (77°F) with a soil-warming pad.

ABOVE AND RIGHT

Until the early 1940s, *Metasequoia glyptostroboides*, commonly known as the dawn redwood, was thought to be extinct, known only through fossil records. In about 1943, Professor Zhan Wang collected a specimen in western Hubei Province in China which at first was thought to belong to the genus *Glyptostrobus*. By 1945, botanists at National Central University in Nanking, China, had realized that it was a plant never seen before and after further study the discovery of *Metasequoia glyptostroboides* was announced. The species is the only member of the genus *Metasequoia* and is a deciduous pine, making it one of the very few conifers that sheds its leaves. In 1948 the tree was introduced to the West, and was first cultivated at Kew. Since that time, the dawn redwood has been propagated in large numbers; it grows rapidly from cuttings in warm climates, and some specimens have been known to reach 40m (131ft) in height. Today, the specimen that was planted at Kew Gardens in 1949 measures a height of 16m (52 1/2 ft).

BIBLIOGRAPHY

Barron, W., *The British Winter Garden*. Bradbury and Evans, London 1852

Blunt, Wilfrid, *In for a Penny: A Prospect of Kew Gardens, their Flora, Fauna and Falballas*. Hamish Hamilton, London 1978

Briggs, Roy, *'Chinese' Wilson: A Life of Ernest H. Wilson 1876-1930*. HMSO, London 1993

Curtis's Botanical Magazine, Volume 80, tab 4773, 1854

Curtis's Botanical Magazine, Volume 117, tab 7153, 1891

Desmond, Ray, *The History of the Royal Botanic Gardens, Kew*, 2nd edition. Royal Botanic Gardens, Kew, London 2007

Desmond, Ray, *Sir Joseph Dalton Hooker: Traveller and Plant Collector*. Antique Collectors' Club, Woodbridge, Suffolk 1999

Desmond, Ray & Hepper, F. Nigel, *A century of Kew Plantsmen: A celebration of the Kew Guild*. Royal Botanic Gardens, Kew. Kew Guild, Kew 1993

Drayton, Richard, *Nature's Government: Science, Imperial Britain and the Improvement of the World*. Yale University Press, New Haven & London 2000

Endersby, Jim, *Imperial Nature: Joseph Hooker and the practices of Victorian science*, University of Chicago Press, Chicago 2008

Hutchinson's Genera of Flowering Plants. (1965, May) *Taxon*, 14 (5): 166-8

Fry, Carolyn, *The Plant Hunters: The adventures of the world's greatest botanical explorers*. Andre Deutsch, London, in Association with the Royal Botanic Gardens, Kew, 2012

Griffiths, John, *Tea: The drink that changed the world*. Andre Deutsch, London 2007

Halliwell, Brian, (1982), A History of the Kew Rock Gardens, *Royal Botanic Gardens Newsletter*, 167: 4-6

Jinshuang Ma, (2003), The Chronology of the 'Living Fossil' *Metasequoia glyptostroboides* (Taxodiaceae): A Review (1943-2003), Harvard Papers in Botany, 8 (1): 9

Hepper, F. Nigel, *Royal Botanic Gardens, Kew: Gardens for Science and Pleasure*. H.M.S.O., London 1982

Indian Tea Gazette Editor, *The Tea Cyclopaedia*: Articles on tea, tea science, blights, soils and manures.. etc with tea statistics. W.B. Whittingham & Co, London 1882

The Kew Guild, *The Journal of the Kew Guild*: Royal Botanic Gardens, Kew

Kingdon-Ward, Francis, *Return to the Irrawaddy*. A. Melrose, London 1956

Kingdon-Ward, Jean, *My Hill So Strong*, Cape, London 1952

Lewis, Gwilym, *Postcards from Kew*. Royal Botanic Gardens, Kew, H.M.S.O., London 1989

Lewis, Jan, *Walter Hood Fitch, A celebration*. HMSO, London 1992

Lyte, Charles, *Frank Kingdon-Ward: Last of the great plant hunters*. John Murray, London 1989

McCracken, Donal, *Gardens of Empire: Botanical institutions of the Victorian British Empire*. Leicester University Press, London 1997

Major, Graham, *Custodians of Kew*. Royal Botanic Gardens, Kew, London 1998

Minter, Sue, *The Greatest Glass House: the rainforests recreated*. H.M.S.O., London 1990

Moon, Debra, *History of the Hooker Oak*. City of Chico, Chico, California 2005

Soviet Scientific Work on Potatoes. (1942, 17th October), *Nature*, 150: 456-7

North, Marianne, *Recollections of a Happy Life: Being the autobiography of Marianne North*. Macmillan, London 1892

Pearson, M. B., *Richard Spruce: Naturalist and explorer*. Hudson History, Settle 2004

Ridley, Henry, *Spices*. Macmillan, London 1912

Royal Botanic Gardens, Kew, *Jodrell Laboratory Centenary 1876-1976*. Unpublished pamphlet, printed 1976

Royal Botanic Gardens, Kew, *Kew Bulletin*, 1892 & various volumes

Royal Botanic Gardens, Kew, *Official Guide to the Museums of Economic Botany, No 1*. Her Majesty's Stationery Office, London 1907

Royal Botanic Gardens, Kew, *Report on the Progress and Condition of the Royal Gardens at Kew, during the year 1877*, Her Majesty's Stationery Office, London 1878

Sethuraj, M, *Natural Rubber: Biology, Cultivation and Technology*. Elsevier, Amsterdam 1992

Smith, F. Porter, *Chinese Materia Medica: Vegetable kingdom*. Printed at the American Presbyterian mission press, Shanghai 1871

Seward, M. & Fitzgerald, Sylvia (eds), *Richard Spruce 1817-1893: Botanist and Explorer*. Royal Botanic Gardens, Kew, London 1996

Tennent, Alan, *British Merchant Ships sunk by U-Boats in World War One*. Starling Press, Newport, Gwent 1990

Thiselton-Dyer, William, *Botanical Enterprise of the Empire*. Printed by Eyre and Spottiswoode for Her Majesty's Stationery Office, London 1880.

Wickens, Gerald (1993). Two centuries of Economic Botanists at Kew Part 1. *Curtis's Botanical Magazine*, 10 (2): 84-93.

ARCHIVE RESOURCES

A number of sources from the Archive Collections of the Royal Botanic Gardens, Kew were consulted, including the following:

Miscellaneous Reports: MR/149 India. Economic Products. Tea c. 1875- 1903; MR/449 Gambia Botanic Station 1880 – 1898; MR/560 Lodoicea Sechellarum 1827 - 1902

Directors' Correspondence Volume 199, United States Letters (South & West), 1865-1900, folio 318: Letter from Muir to Hooker addressed and dated Martinez Contra Costa Co. California, Feb 20th 1882; Folios 322-323 Letters from Eadweard Muybridge to Hooker

Joseph Hooker Papers: JDH/2/16, Letters to William Thiselton-Dyer

Papers of RBGK during the Second World War, WWK/2: Ministry of Agriculture and Fisheries memo to all A.R.P. Personnel

Registered File 1/ADM/41 *Kew Publicity*: Letter from Sir Edward Salisbury, Director of RBG, Kew to CT Houghton, MAFF, dated 29/11/1952

Registered File QE0140 *Maintenance of Palm House - General & General Correspondence: Kew's Contribution to the War Effort*, Ministry of Agriculture press release dated 10th November 1943

Registered File QG416 *Sir Isaac Newton's Apple Tree*

William Dallimore Papers: A Gardener's Reminiscences, including 45 years on the Staff of the Royal Botanic Gardens, Kew, c1950s

John Lindley Papers: Report on the State and Condition of the Royal Gardens, 1838

SOURCES FROM ELSEWHERE

Hooker, William Jackson to Talbot, William Henry Fox, 15 February 1848, Doc. No.: 6109, Fox Talbot Collection, British Library, London

PICTURE REFERENCES AND CREDITS

Front cover: From Kew's collection. Image taken by Nigel Hepper

All images © The Board of Trustees of the Royal Botanic Gardens, Kew unless otherwise stated below. The publisher would like to thank the sources below for their kind permission to reproduce images. Every effort has been made to acknowledge correctly and contact the source and/or copyright holders. The Royal Botanic Gardens, Kew and the publisher apologise for any unintentional errors or omissions and would be grateful to be notified of any corrections, which will be incorporated in future editions.

HNR: Henry Ridley Papers (RBG Kew Archives)
KGU: Kew Guild Collection (RBG Kew Archives)
ROS: Reginald Rose-Innes Papers (RBG Kew Archives)
FKW: Frank Kingdon-Ward Papers (RBG Kew Archives)
AWH: Arthur Hill Papers (RBG Kew Archives)
EHW: Ernest Henry Wilson (RBG Library)

Images from the Frank Kingdon-Ward Papers are copyright / reproduced with kind permission of the Royal Geographic Society.

Chapter 2

39, 50 EHW; 52, Gardens rockery HNR/1/2/6/6, Singapore Herbarium HNR/1/2/1/14; 53 EHW (both); 60, MR/449 Miscellaneous Report Gambia Botanic Station 1880-1898, folio 173

Chapter 3

65 EHW; 70, Wollaston HNR/1/4; 71, Snowden and tent KGU/1/9/3/40; 72, Ridley on foot HNR/1/2/9/66; 73, Sedan chair KGU/1/9/3/42, Arthur Hill on horse in Bolivia AWH/4/1; 74, Ridley with a boat HNR/1/2/6/5, EHW; 75, Rose-Innes in car ROS/4/2/10; 76, Rose-Innes with campfire ROS/4/2/10; 77, Rose-Innes in desert ROS/4/8; 78, Snowden group shot KGU/1/9/3/43, Frank and Jean Kingdon-Ward FKW/1/38; 80, Turrill with a vasculum KGU/1/9/3/39; 82, Jean on mountainside FKW/3/4/3, Blue poppy FKW/3/4/4, Bridge crossing FKW/3/6; 83, Jean being carried over the river FKW/3/6, Jean with plant FKW/3/4/2; 84-89 all images EHW; 90, Overlooking the lake ROS/4/1/17; 91, Men on mountain ROS/4/1/18, Amongst the plants ROS/4/1/18.

Chapter 4

93, 94, 95, 96 (Victoria Gate and Lion Gate from the Main Road), 98 Queen Charlotte's Cottage, 99, 101 images of the Dripping Well, 103, 104, 105, 106 the Pavilion, 111 Joey the crane, all from the RBG Kew Postcard collection; 102, Japanese Gateway RBG Kew Archives: Kew Pleasure Gardens folio 150; 107, Waitresses reproduced courtesy of Sylvia Shirley; 108, Forenoon Opening, RBG Kew Archives, folio 216: QX Collections.

Chapter 5

121, Air layering KGU/1/9/3/14, Propagating KGU/1/9/3/34 © Fox Photos; 124, Horses with snow plough reproduced courtesy of the Appleby family; 124,125, reproduced courtesy of Wendy Pollard; 127, Three female gardeners and Annie Gulvin KGU/1/9/3/262; 134, KGU/1/9/2/199; 135, John Hutchinson KGU/1/9/3/22; 135, Two women in mounting room © Bersen's International Press Service; 136, lower right, Stella Ross-Craig; 137, Ann Webster © RBG Kew Archives, taken by Francis Ballard; 138, KGU/1/9/3/31; 140, KGU/1/9/1/112; 141, Wood Museum © Keystone; 142, Kew Guild dinner KGU/1/9/1/112; 143, Tea party KGU/1/9/3/3, Botany club, Nigel Hepper Collection; 144, Tennis club KGU/1/9/1/129; 145, Football club KGU/1/9/1/42; 147, Demo Plot © Fox Photos.

Chapter 6

149, J. B. Reardon KGU/1/9/2/88, Frank KGU/1/9/2/142; 153, Herbarium with sandbags / 154, First Aid Station photograph, 155, WB Turril dressed in gas suit, all © RBG Kew taken by Francis Ballard; 157, Seed demonstration KGU/1/9/3/7; 160, © Keystone; 161, Land girls KGU/1/9/1/130, M.R.F. Taylor KGU/1/9/2/45 taken by Francis Ballard; 162, 163, women gardeners, © Keystone; 164, Woman pruning blossoms © Illustrated; 165 right, 166, 167, 168, 169, 170 women gardeners, all © Keystone; 171, © Women's Illustrated; 172, J.W. Sutch KGU/1/9/2/43, A.K. Jackson KGU/1/9/2/49; 172, Bomb damage, Kew Road, reproduced by kind permission of Richmond Local History Library, from their collections.

Chapter 7

176, Australia House © Fox Photos / 178, AEFAT Conference, Nigel Hepper Collection / 181 KGU/1/9/3/6; 188 KGU/1/9/3/6 / 190, 191 RBG Kew School of Horticulture Slide Collections / 191, Scarecrow KGU/1/9/2/115; 192, 193, Student photo album, RBG Kew Archives: QX Collections / 194, 1969 Intake graduation KGU/1/9/3/97, with kind permission from Alan Titchmarsh / 204, images of 1960s germination © and kind permission of John Simmons, 1970 germination © and kind permission of Stewart Henchie.